Page 3 Politics

Alleged political views of The Sun's topless
models under editor Rebekah Wade/Brooks
(from 'News in Briefs' 2003-2009)

Tim Ireland

For Justin

Page Three girls are intelligent, vibrant young women who appear in the Sun out of choice and because they enjoy the job.

Unsurprisingly, millions of our readers - men and women - enjoy looking at them.

Rebekah Wade
Editorial (extract)
The Sun, 14 January 2004

"I've asked my source at News International [about 'News in Briefs']... and my source says the deputy editor who's in charge of Page 3 decides the topic and then one of the subs writes it. The girls have nothing whatsoever to do with it, because apart from the one with a degree, they're as daft they look."

Olly Mann
'Answer Me This' podcast
00:21:25 | Ep 168 | 24 February 2011

CONTENTS

The
loveliest
girls
are
always
in The
Sun

A swell pair of puppies

★ FETCHING lovely Karen, 20, sends the local boys barking when she romps with her puppies in the park. She has two naughty spaniels who chase everything but the stick.

★ But life isn't all that ruff. We hear that she gets plenty of wolf-whistles, too.

Picture Credit
PHOTOGRAPHER

Mock-up of layout/content of a typical Page 3 feature, circa 1972-1997

Introduction

Once upon a time, there were tits on page 3 of nearly every edition of an otherwise rabidly conservative tabloid owned by Rupert Murdoch, and for one brief, shining moment in the noughties, there was something about this that was even more extraordinary.

Apparently, it all started innocently enough one day in 1969, when Murdoch bought an ailing newspaper called The Sun and reinvented it as a populist tabloid complete with a picture of a clothed glamour model on page 3 to 'brighten one's day'. Those who tell the story are often keen to point out that this next part happened on a day when Rupert Murdoch had stepped out overseas for a moment (on 17 November 1970), but within a year those lovely ladies were topless, and not long after that, reliably so.

Page 3 was born on this day, and boobs in 'red top' tabloids soon became the norm.

The Golden Age

The Sun quickly evolved a 'look' for Page 3 that was solid by the early 70s and continued uninterrupted for more than twenty years, well into the 90s. Using a widely-deployed method of helping readers to better identify with strange women in magazines (see: Playboy models and their list of 'likes' and 'dislikes'), the topless ladies on Page 3 were accompanied by a small pun-filled caption based on that model's alleged interests.

Heavy use of double entendres allowed The Sun to include both insight and innuendo in these captions, enabling the average male to identify with the model while still keeping in mind the whole point of the exercise: to objectify her sexually in order to 'brighten one's day'.

For example, were the model training to be an accountant, the text would playfully refer to her "ample assets" and the "bottom line," fnarr-fnarr. Had the model been a vet's assistant or even merely the owner of a small domestic animal, the caption would suggest that "She also brings the beast out in us, eh readers?"... and so on and so forth until you feared your sides would split.

This feature was quietly edited away just before the turn of the century like the anachronism it was (as Page 3 itself would be some 15 years later), and so Page 3 drifted as a blank canvas until one day in early 2003 when a lady named Rebekah Wade (later 'Brooks') took over as editor and decided that Page 3 would not be done away with under a female editor as many expected, but would instead be transformed into a nationwide political platform for all comers with two X chromosomes and a nice pair of tits.

Mock-up of layout/content of a typical Page 3 feature, circa 2003-2009

The ~~Propaganda~~ Political Age

Slowly at first, and mainly passing judgement on minor piffles and wayward celebs in those early months, Page 3 became the regular home of a new feature titled 'News in Briefs': a short editorial in the name of whoever was showing their tits off on that day. This editorial was enclosed in a stylised inverted apostrophe that was reminiscent of a comic-book 'speech balloon', often placed near or above the model's head, adding to the message that readers were witness to the immediate and true voice of the model in question.

By late 2003, these editorials were increasingly political, and often deeply so. Most of the politics involved was domestic (and notably insular), and very little was said about world affairs, unless it was on the subject of war and/or terrorism.

Page 3 continued in this vein throughout the editorship of Rebekah Wade/Brooks. When Dominic Mohan took over as editor in late 2009, 'News in Briefs' descended into a pathetic attempt at self-parody that clung to Page 3 like the stench of its approaching death. 'News in Briefs' was retired in June 2013 when David Dinsmore took over, and Page 3 later died in humiliating ignominy on his watch (January 2015).

It was only under Rebekah Wade/Brooks that models on Page 3 appeared next to what appeared to be strong and sincerely-held political opinions (often in support of that day's main editorial), and all of the samples in this book are from her tenure.

Empowerment or Exploitation?

Now, I know what you're thinking, and yes it is unlikely that a young glamour model might spontaneously offer an independent view on a deadly conflict in a foreign country while having ice applied to her nipples to keep them erect under the warm lights of the photographer's studio (i.e. before appearing topless in the next day's newspaper alongside that same politically-charged statement). However, we are obliged to give The Sun the benefit of the doubt on many fronts for several reasons, so here goes:

Obviously, the lovely ladies of Page 3 were photographed weeks if not months in advance of any given appearance. Sometimes, two photos from the same shoot would be used months apart. Further, appearances of finished and finalised photos would have been scheduled days if not weeks in advance, with only scant room for variation at the discretion of the editor, as you'd expect from a daily newspaper.

This being the case, if we are to take The Sun at their word about issues ranging from female empowerment to editorial integrity, the best situation one could hope for here is a model being contacted the day before publication, provided with advance knowledge of the leading stories in the next days' edition, and given a choice of her topic before she is quickly interviewed by phone or email, and her response is finalised as an approved editorial in her name.

(The ideal situation overall involves contacting a qualified expert about the leading topic of the day, obtaining a balanced and informed response from said expert, and then asking them if they wouldn't mind getting their tits out... but the logistics of photography alone would be a nightmare.)

The Cynical View: Soft Pornography as Propaganda

The deeply cynical view would be that these women had no voice on Page 3 worth speaking of, were frequently if not always exploited as mouthpieces for the editor and/or owner of the newspaper, and further were not given much choice about it.

This would be equally worrying and hilarious if it were the case.

There was demonstrable collusion between The Sun and Downing Street (and the Home Office) at the peak of these editorials, and several Page 3 editorials were in line with a government/department policy at a time when the editor had a secret agreement or some other form of undisclosed agenda leading to their newspaper's support of it.

Even if they were not fully informed/aware of any deceit over credit for editorial content on Page 3, it could not have escaped the attention of Tony Blair or any key member of his administration that their private agreement with The Sun included the occasional use of soft porn to push the Blair agenda. Given the structure of the device, at times their own talking points are likely to have appeared on Page 3 as if a topless model's moment of insight were the point of origin.

Holding to the cynical view just long enough to explore how dark this can get, and assuming you'll pardon the odd bit of anecdotal, I have personally witnessed a man in a pub parroting the opinion that appeared on that day's Page 3 as if it were his own. It was near word for word, and exactly the result you would get if a similarly impressionable person had heard that opinion from a friend they respected.

Previously, if a Sun reader wanted to better identify with the model on Page 3, they only needed to read the saucy caption about her life as a vet's assistant. In such a case, perhaps in an effort to further brighten their morning, they might even briefly imagine meeting the girl as they take their poorly tortoise in for a check-up.

However, under the Wade/Brooks regime, you have to take a political viewpoint on board if you want to so much as picture yourself talking to the pretty topless girl with a nice smile and some seemingly sensible things to say about our country being invaded by foreigners and our fun being spoiled by killjoy PC thugs. That changes things; it makes Page 3 a potential and insidious political weapon.

The cynical view contends that this potential was realised in The Sun from 2003 to 2009, as a well-established and notably intimate connection was exploited to gain the trust of readers on political issues, while simultaneously betraying their trust; that the editor wished to influence readers surreptitiously &/or add weight to their own opinions/assertions by repeating them in the voice of that day's topless model.

Basically, treating Page 3 like an Orwellian puppet show with tits.

Editorials on Page 3 *did* sometimes appear to be influenced by how confident Rebekah Wade/Brooks was feeling at the time: after a stinging defeat (like over the 90 day detention vote, see Page 65), 'News in Brief' editorials would disappear from Page 3 for days or even weeks at a time, as if the poor dear had lost her spunk.

Further, when 'News in Briefs' eventually returned to Page 3, the speech-bubble-styled editorials often first re-appeared next to the legs or lower torso of the model before eventually rising to usual prominent location near the head. Now, I could have been imagining most if not all of this, but at times it honestly appeared as if the Page 3 models were not entirely happy about having somebody else's spunk on their page, and certainly not near their face.

And *that* is how dark the cynical view can get, which is why we are going to go forward from this point on giving the fine, upstanding and law-abiding editor Rebekah Wade/Brooks the benefit of the doubt to the extent of assuming good faith on all fronts:

The Trusting View: Page 3 as an Empowering Platform

We are to assume from this moment on that all models have appeared as scheduled, and been approached for their thoughts on their choice of subject, as all Page 3 girls would expect under such a regime (i.e. if a photo from your latest topless shoot were appearing in an upcoming edition, you would be anticipating the call about what you wanted to say on the resulting Page 3 on the day before publication).

We are to further assume that the models have been allowed to speak their mind without any influence from on high, and that they've experienced little to no fear of retribution for expressing strong views, or even for engaging in outright abuse.

Consequently, the generous view puts it that each model 'owns' the relevant opinions and contentions published in their name, and therefore takes responsibility for these statements apparently made of their own free will.

The alternative is to acknowledge the existence of an ugly conspiracy to exploit women and deceive readers for political gain.

I trust that we are on the same page, both literally and figuratively.

OK, you're about as ready as one can manage in the few short pages we've had to get to know each other, so prepare to dive in to a world where pretty young ladies get their jugs out to weigh in on the big political issues of the day.

I'll be right by your side to put some of the more obscure, enigmatic or downright misleading entries into context, and to keep reminding you of the importance of giving the good people at The Sun the benefit of the doubt at all times.

The BBC

The Sun's generally hostile position on the BBC is widely documented. It is also easy to appreciate what Rupert Murdoch personally stands to gain from any damage to the credibility, success and/or funding of this major news and broadcast rival. Further, during the noughties, the BBC stood as one of the few media bodies daring to question the official narrative of the invasion of Iraq and the scandals and disasters that followed. We'll get to all of that soon enough, but for now let us keep uppermost in our minds the idea that the following stated positions are genuine and unsolicited views of a series of topless models whose photos just happen to be appearing in that day's issue.

06 January 2005

Ruth is reportedly in a state of disbelief that the BBC has chosen to show *Jerry Springer: The Opera,* despite a major campaign against it by a series of moral campaigners (who led the way with some wildly exaggerated claims about the frequency of swear-words by multiplying any instance of the lyric 'fuck' by the number of people in the chorus). Concerned about a perceived wall of swears, Ruth gets her tits out to suggest that more wholesome fare might be appropriate to fill a perceived 'gap' in Saturday night entertainment:

> "I'm not surprised they've had complaints about the swearing. Why can't they plug the Saturday night telly gap with good sitcoms or quiz shows instead?"
>
> *Ruth (22, from Kent)*

24 May 2005

On 23 May, BBC staff who were members of the unions Amicus, BECTU and NUJ staged a 24-hour strike over redundancy plans. The strike caused notable disruption to television & radio services, particularly news output. The next day, fresh-faced Keeley is described as being 'surprised' to see the BBC disrupted by the strike, and adds:

> "I can't imagine too many people noticed anyway."
>
> *Keeley (18, from Bromley)*

Of course, there's absolutely no evidence that the competing interests of Sky News and BBC News played any role in the genesis of this needlessly disparaging but ostensibly off-the-cuff remark. I want to be clear on that point.

12 October 2005

We are told that Becky is "appalled" at news that the BBC wants to charge her more for a TV licence, and she goes on to express concern on behalf of licence-payers as a whole, saying:

> "The Beeb should cut spending for things like meals and taxis before charging us more to watch."

Becky (22, from London)

29 October 2008

On Saturday 18 October 2008, an edition of *The Russell Brand Show* (BBC Radio 2) featured Russell Brand and Jonathan Ross attempting to call the actor Andrew Sachs for a scheduled on-air interview, before leaving a series of lewd messages on his answering machine. Here, Rosie bares her breasts to offer her personal view of their "crude phone stunt" and echoes calls for both men to be sacked:.

> "They are both talented men, but this was too much. They couldn't complain if the BBC gave them the boot."

Rosie (18, from Surrey)

23 January 2009

Ross has been suspended from the BBC for nearly 3 months, but tonight he returns with a new edition of *Friday Night with Jonathan Ross* (BBC One) and Sam uses the opportunity to remind viewers why his show has been off the air. Expressing hope that Ross has "learned his lesson from the Andrew Sachs row," Sam goes on to say:

> "I missed his show, now let's hope he makes a fresh start."

Sam (23, from Manchester)

26 June 2009

When tabloids were up in arms about 'Sachsgate' and demanding that someone Do Something Immediately, BBC director general Mark Thompson cut short a family holiday to Do Something Immediately. Today, topless model Peta is described as being "furious" on behalf of all BBC licence-payers about the relevant expenses claim for unscheduled flights, then struggles to understand why ending a family holiday involves bringing all of the family members home:

> "Why did we have to fork out for his family as well? It's crazy."

Peta (22, from Essex)

Benefits

Benefits recipients are a favourite target of tabloids. Most tabloid readers already have a sense if not a certainty that they have been cheated all of their lives, but rather than go after anyone of consequence, it is far easier for a tabloid to go after people who cannot defend themselves and imply that *they* are draining society to such an extent that it explains every economic challenge we face. Further, the act of constantly matching the words 'cheat' and/or 'scrounger' to 'benefits' fits their wider conservative agenda for welfare reform (see also: 'illegal' and 'asylum seekers' for immigration reform) .

I will reiterate here that it is possibly down to coincidence and coincidence alone that no Page 3 model has ever run counter to this editorial position. It is equally possible that it is down to sheer chance that no Page 3 model has spoken out against the injustice of targeting some of the most vulnerable people in our society because their editor doesn't have the will/courage to go after those who have cost the public far more than even the most extreme example(s) of benefits fraud.

20 July 2004

We begin, fittingly enough, with the seemingly perfect storm of asylum seekers who did something illegal before going on to claim benefits.

In February 2000, nine Afghan men fleeing the Taliban regime hijacked a scheduled domestic flight in Afghanistan and forced the crew to fly to Stansted Airport in the UK, leading to a days-long siege involving 180 passengers and a conviction for hijacking and false imprisonment. That conviction was later quashed and subsequent attempts to return the men to Afghanistan were prevented by the Human Rights Act (also known in tabloids as 'the hated Human Rights Act' and 'the so-called Human Rights Act').

The Sun ran a sustained campaign of condemnation in the years it took to get to this point, but by now all legal arguments to have the men imprisoned or deported have been exhausted, so today it is up to Charlotte to make a fresh case to the public that "Afghan hijackers are living a comfortable life in Britain" - in nice houses, no less - and she is quoted as saying:

> "I can understand why they wanted to flee from the Taliban - but the Taliban have now been ousted. These people are on benefits in nice houses with the taxpayer footing the bill."

> *Charlotte (19, from Ipswich)*

I can assure you that we have a long way to go with many further examples on the subject of immigration & terrorism to come, but for now, let's get back to benefits:

16 August 2004

Melanie flashes the sweetest of smiles and allegedly backs calls for the government to "get tough of benefit cheats" by saying:

> "I am staggered how they are ripping off the country.
> The Government should come down very hard on
> anyone making fraudulent claims."

> *Melanie (22, from Watford)*

23 May 2005

Nikkala is said to be "shocked" about a Sun story describing "three teenage sisters, all with children and living on benefits". Obviously concerned that they may lack a suitable topless role model, she exposes her pert but full breasts and gives voice to a lone, lamenting query:

> "Has no one talked to them about taking responsibility?"

> *Nikkala (23, from Middlesex)*

There is no record of what (if any) advice Nikkala intended to share with teenage mothers short on cash and/or career prospects, but it's fun to speculate.

09 January 2008

At this point in time, The Sun are almost two years away from formally endorsing Cameron (under editor Dominic Mohan) but obviously that doesn't stop Page 3 models from speaking their mind on topics that just happen to be in line with The Sun's long-standing views on benefits. Today, Rhian is reportedly "delighted" by Tory leader David Cameron's vow to "tackle benefit scroungers" and says:

> "It's about time someone sorted them out."

> *Rhian (21, from Manchester)*

17 March 2008

The Sun claims some UK-based families "are collecting £30,000 a year in benefits," and we are told by Keeley that this "scandal" warrants immediate investigation:

> "Hard-working parents are earning less than those who sit at
> home and get handouts. And that is not even taking into
> account the cost of childcare. It should be investigated."

> *Keeley (21, from Bromley)*

08 October 2008

Citing what cynics might describe as a far-from-typical example, Danni expresses her surprise at the idea that someone might get "a £1.2million mansion on state benefits".

While the reported 15K per month in rent paid to a private landlord does seem excessive to host even the largest of families, one wonders why anyone would risk giving people the false impression that some asylum seekers then get to keep the house... but let's not let that minor detail distract us from what a topless model may or may not think about what may or may not be happening here:

> "It takes lots of hard work to afford a place like that.
> It's crazy some people can get it for free."

> *Danni (21, from Coventry)*

08 December 2008

The government has since February been airing plans for improvements to the immigration process, and what catches Nikkala's eye today is the proviso that those in the earliest stages of the process should not be entitled to benefits until a 'probationary period' has passed:

> "The country has to tighten its belt, and can't afford to hand
> out benefits to everyone as soon as they arrive in Britain."

> *Nikkala (25, from Middlesex)*

30 July 2009

Rosie is "appalled" by Theresa Winters, dubbed the "baby machine" by tabloids after having over a dozen children, all of whom ended up in care. Some might spare a moment of sympathy for Winters, who aspired to be a good parent but struggled with responsibility. Others might prefer to spare a thought for the many children involved, four of whom were born with PEHO syndrome (an extremely rare degenerative condition that leads to a loss of eyesight, painful swelling and progressive brain dysfunction). However, today we are assured that Rosie is mainly if not only concerned about what this is costing her personally in cash terms:

> "She shouldn't have any more children. She's clearly
> not capable of looking after them. They all end up in
> care, and it's not fair on the rest of us who have to pay
> a fortune to support them all."

> *Rosie (18, from Middlesex)*

26 August 2009

Rebekah Wade/Brooks announced her retirement from The Sun earlier this month, and on this day Dominic Mohan was named as her successor. The official changeover took place in the first days of September but what you are looking at here is the last example of a Page 3 editorial under Wade/Brooks... i.e. before all of the models suddenly and inexplicably changed their minds and decided that they wanted to be the subject of the same 'dumb bird with her tits out' joke again and again for years to come.

Today, Sam is reportedly shocked to hear about two million Brits having never done a day's work, choosing instead to live on benefits. Apparently.

> "It's particularly depressing for those of us who work
> hard for a living and spend our whole lives shelling out
> thousands to support them."
>
> *Sam (23, from Manchester)*

Crime & Punishment

Have you ever watched *The Jeremy Kyle Show* or any exploitative trash like it and felt glad that - for all your faults - you weren't as bad as the target of that day's episode? Did you enjoy watching a hate figure 'get what's coming to them', or feel the glorious rush of ranting against the injustice when they didn't? That's the primary attraction of crime reporting for tabloid readers. For tabloid *producers*, it mainly comes down to keeping their readers in a constant state of fear and reliance. That sense of reliance is reinforced by the tabloid appearing to wage a constant battle against the forces of evil and campaigning for the government/police to get tough on 'real criminals' (i.e. instead of motorists, and so-called journalists hacking the voicemail messages of dead teenage girls).

Crime

03 December 2003

We are told that Zoe is "not surprised" by figures apparently showing "90 per cent of crimes never result in a conviction". I find it very surprising myself; how do they know that all of the alleged acts were crimes if there were no convictions? Anyway, we are assured that Zoe said the following in response to the alleged findings:

> "Street crime is so common nowadays that the police have a tough job catching crooks. It's a very sad state of affairs for this country - and it doesn't look like it's getting any better."

Zoe (22, from London)

23 January 2004

In January 2004, cannabis laws were relaxed but the drug remained illegal. To make sure this message got across clearly, the government invested in radio advertisements to be carried on 48 national and regional stations in a campaign designed to reach 80% of British teenagers... but somehow they missed Corina (19, from Oxford). Today, Corina appears to say that "new cannabis laws are a shambles" and follows this with:

> "The whole issue has been a complete fiasco and handled very badly. You don't need to smoke something funny to be in a haze of confusion over it."

Corina (19, from Oxford)

16 July 2004

Today we are assured that Ruthie is wholly in support of a plan to air court hearings on television - i.e. like the aforementioned Jeremy Kyle vehicle, with prison sentences - but for some reason she avoids the obvious comparison, and instead chooses to go with soap operas:

> "It'll be great entertainment as well as making the justice system clearer for most of us. A lot of cases would have people glued to the screens - it could rival Corrie and Eastenders."
>
> *Ruthie (22, from Kent)*

13 December 2004

Child molestation was a demonstrable obsession for editor Rebekah Wade/Brooks, resulting in a many in-house campaigns chasing alleged serial predators (precisely none of which resulted in consequences for beloved child entertainers Jimmy Savile and Rolf Harris) but today Kerri is reportedly "shocked" at figures showing "the number of children who come under attack from carers" and adorns her message with suitably grim tinsel:

> "At Christmas, most kids are looking forward to unwrapping gifts. But we forget many are living in fear. It's time the Government did more to help them."
>
> *Kerri (18, from London)*

Merry Christmas, readers!

14 December 2004

The 'Knives Destroy Lives' campaign is calling for a 5-year minimum sentence for anyone carrying a blade longer than 3 inches. The initiative is led by former police officer Norman Brennan under the charity 'Victims of Crime Trust' and you're encouraged to Google both names for further context. For now, all you need to know is that The Sun's editor is totally on board, and by sheer coincidence, so too is that day's topless model. In fact, rather than mess about with any silly nonsense about blade length, Neval calls for "anyone caught carrying a blade" to be given a 5-year jail term and reportedly says:

> "The Knives Destroy Lives campaign speaks for itself. It's time the law was changed, because violent crime is out of control. The Government needs to let the public know it's doing something about it."
>
> *Neval (21, from London)*

03 February 2005

Today, Katie praises the government for "making clear the rights of homeowners to defend themselves against burglary". This is a surprisingly sophisticated ploy from a random glamour model, given the circumstances. Allow me to explain...

Tory backbenchers have triggered a debate on amending the law regarding the acceptable use of force one might use against an intruder, despite the Labour government repeatedly making it clear that they have no plans to change it. The law as it stands allows "reasonable force" to be used against an intruder, but the challengers want to allow everything up to "grossly disproportionate force" and claim that the current law is too confusing.

To combat any alleged confusion, the Association of Chief Police Officers and the Crown Prosecution Service have issued advice in the form of a pamphlet to explain what "reasonable force" is... basically, anything up to disproportionate force, because dictionary. Why certain Conservative backbenchers are calling for allowances to be made up to "*grossly* disproportionate force" is anybody's guess, but what really matters in this context is the girl with her tits out backing the government and praising their advice while simultaneously appearing to hold the view of those seeking to give intruders a jolly good kicking. It's very cunning:

> "Any other policy is madness. Break into a home and you break the law. Police should always side with the victim."

> *Katie (19, from Liverpool)*

29 March 2005

Budget cuts have resulted in changes to police training, and not enough of it is basic enough for 'superfit' Krystle, who wants a return to "tough workouts":

> "It's madness. Young thugs will be easily able to outrun a couple of unfit bobbies. On top of that, flabby officers won't look so good in uniform."

> *Krystle (22, from Manchester)*

12 April 2005

A classic of the genre from Becky, who we are told does not approve of a new points system for traffic police, calling it an "own goal":

> "They need to be clamping down on real criminals, not giving motorists a hard time."

> *Becky (24, from London)*

08 June 2005

Keeley puffs out her ample chest and demands a "blitz on phone bullies".

No, not the kind who are illicitly accessing the voicemails of celebrities, politicians and murdered schoolgirls... the other, more dangerous kind:

> "How can anyone get enjoyment from this? People caught happy slapping or sending sick txt messages should be hauled before the courts."
>
> *Keeley (18, from Bromley)*

28 February 2007

And the 'real mobile phone criminals' keep on coming!

On this day, Becky is described as being "appalled" by recent statistics about the number of drivers using mobile phones while driving:

> "Using your mobile phone while driving makes you four more times likely to have a crash. I back the new penalties - it's high time we hit these selfish idiots where it hurts."
>
> *Becky (24, from London)*

16 October 2007

The government has been listening to concerns from senior judges about mandatory sentences filling overcrowded prisons with "geriatric lifers" (i.e. instead of having terms of imprisonment reflect any actual risk to the public).

The lord chief justice, Lord Phillips, said earlier in the year:

> *"I detect on the part of (some) publications an incitement to the public to exact vengeance from offenders that is not dissimilar from the emotions of those who thronged to witness public executions in the 18th century."*

Sadly, we can only guess at who he was talking about.

Anyway, today we are informed that topless model Danni is "outraged" by government plans to allow "shorter sentences (for) dangerous, violent criminals" and further assured that she said this in response:

> "It's a crazy idea. These people should be locked away for as long as possible."
>
> *Danni (21, from Coventry)*

09 July 2008

On a similar theme, here we are told that Ruth is "furious" about recent government recommendations that will allow burglars to "dodge jail with community sentences":

> "This sends the wrong message and is hardly a deterrent."
>
> *Ruth (25, from Kent)*

15 August 2008

Nikkala is apparently worried by figures showing a "soaring number of drug deaths in Britain" and urges us to please think of the children. Stay away from drugs, kids. You might die.

> "More must be done to stop young people getting drawn into drug abuse."
>
> *Nikkala (24, from Middlesex)*

22 October 2008

Zoe is reportedly "amazed" to hear that a drug cartel would break the law by keeping lions and tigers at their mansion and allegedly states the obvious:

> "If these animals had escaped they could have killed people. It was an incredibly dangerous and really irresponsible thing to do."
>
> *Zoe (25, from London)*

Me, I have some added concerns that if these animals were being kept illicitly, then they probably weren't being cared for properly, but whatever. Stay away from drugs cartels, kids. You might die.

24 October 2008

The government has been mistakenly classifying some crimes of "grievous bodily harm with intent" as lesser crimes, leading to an embarrassing admission about recent statistics: overall crime is still down, but violent crime is up. We're told Peta is certain that figures were "tweaked" deliberately to "hide a rise in violent crime" and that this indicates that the whole reporting system can no longer be trusted:

> "How can we trust these official figures ever again now they have been shown to be wrong? I think it's terrible."
>
> *Peta (21, from Essex)*

10 December 2008

The Sentencing Guidelines Council has released new guidelines for judges and magistrates on 'non-dwelling' theft - aka shoplifting - to provide judges with a range of fitting sanctions.

Just to give you a rough idea of the sophistication of the new guidelines: the SGC recommends higher sentences for those who target smaller/independent stores (on the basis that these small enterprises are more vulnerable economically and owners are more likely to suffer greater harm) and minimum 12 month custodial sentences for those who use/threaten harm and/or operate in organised gangs.

However, all The Sun care to talk about is a contingency for substance abusers that amounts to "druggie and alcoholic shoplifters" getting an "easy ride" in their view, and as usual, the Page 3 model is right there telling us how it is... or rather, how the good people at The Sun say it is:

> "This is ridiculously unfair on our hard-working shopkeepers. These sort of offenders need tougher penalties, not softer ones."
>
> *Amii (22, from Birmingham)*

12 December 2008

Danni allegedly urges us not to become complacent in the face of crime statistics (that you can't trust anyway) showing a drop in serious knife crimes and says:

> "It's good news, but there is still a lot of work to do. We've got to get knives off the streets completely."
>
> *Danni (21, from Coventry)*

11 March 2009

Becky is reportedly "stunned" at reports that 1,063 serving police officers have criminal convictions ranging from forgery and assault to theft and (quite an important one, you would think) perverting the course of justice.

I'm totally for the lady with her jugs out on this one, but will note that her point is undermined by her own news organisation's record when it comes to staying on the right side of the law in the pursuit of justice, to say nothing of their personal lives.

> "It's worrying when so many of the people who are meant to uphold the law have broken it themselves. They should all be sacked."
>
> *Becky (25, from London)*

05 May 2009

Annual statistics show that police have issued 1.5 million speeding tickets. Katie is "outraged" by this and says obviously it's illegal to speed, but it's far too easy to get caught these days. OK, so I'm paraphrasing, but...

> "It is just another example of this money-grubbing Government. Obviously, it's illegal to speed but there are far too many cameras on our roads now."

Katie (23, from Liverpool)

14 June 2009

Danni is "staggered" (geddit?) by the scale of boozy rowdiness on Britain's streets:

> "Mindless yobbery, so often fuelled by alcohol, is the blight of modern Britain. This Government has to find a way of cutting levels of anti-social behaviour."

Danni (22, from Coventry)

10 July 2009

You may recall signs of violent knife crime going down in a recent entry. Well, some of that may have something to do with police catching more people carrying knives, I couldn't possibly say. In any case, Nikkala is "shocked" about new figures showing a large number of people being caught with knives and says:

> "We have to get the message across that it's wrong - that it's never cool to carry a knife*."

Nikkala (24, from Middlesex)

(*Unless you're Crocodile Dundee. Obviously.)

17 July 2009

Rhian gives a rousing Page 3 welcome to The Sun's Police Bravery Awards and says:

> "People don't realise the great risks our officers take with their own safety to protect the public from harm. They are the real heroes*."

Rhian (22, from Manchester)

(*Except when they pull you over for speeding. Obviously.)

Prisons

19 January 2004

By now you should have noticed how often the Page 3 ladies are allegedly "shocked" by something, and this entry is no exception, but today Katie is described as being both "shocked" *and* "furious" to hear that Britain's jails are being "blighted by political correctness". Yes, it is *that* serious, and matters are *that* dire. Clearly.

> "Criminals are in prison to be punished. Warders must be able to show they're in charge and not have to pussyfoot around inmates."
>
> *Katie (23, from Coventry)*

20 September 2006

Rather than see prison overcrowding addressed by anything so shocking as sentence/sentencing reviews, the lovely Freya is reportedly "delighted" by talk of a new(ish) prison emerging from a disused Army barracks:

> "People who have been jailed should stay inside until they serve their time - not be let out because there are no more cells. It's good to see these empty camps being used."
>
> *Freya (19, from Nottingham)*

25 February 2008

In one of life's incredible coincidences, both The Sun's editor Rebekah Wade/Brooks and today's Page 3 model have identical views on capital punishment that run counter to their readers' (and most of their writers') expectations.

Amy D, we are told, "can understand why families of murder victims are calling for the return of the death penalty" but seeks to convince them that there are worse punishments than being killed to death, like being locked up "forever" in a prison (albeit one where the warden has to pussyfoot around you):

> "There are so many terrible people stalking the streets, that there has to be a stronger deterrent. They should be locked away forever."
>
> *Amy D (22, from Widnes)*

You'll want to keep this one in mind as we go on to learn how dreadful life is in prison...

26 February 2008

'Stunning' Rhian is "shocked" again, this time at the notion that a convicted drug dealer was allowed to co-pilot an aircraft while on weekend release. I suspect the following joke is based at least in part on assumptions about smuggling:

> "Whatever next? Before we know it, bank robbers
> will be allowed to take Saturday jobs at Barclays. Lags
> get far too easy a ride these days."

Rhian (21, from Manchester)

31 October 2008

Hazelle is described as being "appalled" at the idea that Broadmoor 'dangermen' inmates have been permitted a "fancy-dress Halloween bash" and says:

> "It is in very bad taste. How can it right for them to
> dress up and have a good time?"

Keeley (22, from Bromley)

It later emerged that The Sun had paid an NHS worker £1000 cash for the tip-off that led to a subsequent withdrawal of costume privileges, and as if to rub it in, Hazelle is today pictured dressed up as a witch... and clearly having a good time.

21 November 2008

Amy G reportedly "cannot believe" what she has heard about "a convicted terrorist, murderers and rapists... being taught to tell gags behind bars". This may be because what she has been told (if she has been told anything at all) is somewhat misleading.

18 prisoners signed up to a certificated course with lessons ranging from stand-up comedy to comic drama, improvisation and scriptwriting. That they didn't get much further than rudimentary stand-up is down to Jack Straw reacting to tabloid outrage by pulling the initiative three days in, but it is far easier to upset readers with the idea that prisoners are laughing at them than it is with the idea that they are interpretive-dancing at them.

In any case, today's topless model is so upset, she appears not to understand that (ideally) in stand-up, the audience laughs, not the comic-in-training:

> "It was in very bad taste. These people should be
> paying for their crimes not having a laugh."

Amy G (20, from Sheffield)

29 April 2009

Once again it's reported that Amy G "can't believe" what she has been told, this time about "David Walliams' stalker (being) allowed to 'wed' the Little Britain star".

This follows a report by The Sun that the recently-sectioned Sarah Bartholomew had been permitted a mock wedding ceremony in Kneesworth House Hospital where she played both the bride and the vicar, seemingly after threatening legal action if she did not get her way. I am not sure who, if anyone, was paid for this tabloid tip-off, but I've got good money on Mr Walliams' stand-in.

> "This woman is clearly unwell and I cannot see how this mock ceremony will help her get any better."

> *Amy G (20, from Sheffield)*

Current Events

This section is about events. That were current. At the time.

It's hard to know what else to say about this assorted mish-mash of cheap populism. It is what it is.

Local & National

22 March 2006

Becky declares that "politicians need to clean up their act" if they expect "our votes" and says:

> "The loans-for-peerages row has only made people question the work of the government more."

Becky (24, from London)

07 March 2007

Becky & Mel are in their usual happy clinch, but we are told that they are "outraged" by a phone vote scandal involving a TV network that does not belong to Rupert Murdoch. It is alleged that Becky says:

> "There's few things we love more than to vote on I'm A Celeb, but this takes all the fun out of it."

Becky (24, from London)

21 January 2008

Zoe is reportedly "outraged" about Britain having Europe's highest rail fares.

> "Our train services have always been a national joke - now they're a European one. Commuters are sick of being taken for a ride."

Zoe (26, from London)

24 March 2008

On this day we are assured that Becky "sympathises" with Tessa Jowell after "gipsies moved in just yards from the government minister's home," but it is clear from the tone of the wider coverage that almost everybody at The Sun is laughing at the minister through their hands.

In tabloid world, just as benefits are only ever used by scroungers, the 'so-called' Human Rights Act is only ever used as a cynical ploy by wrongs-uns, such as travellers seeking to frustrate a local council's efforts to eject them from an illicit settlement.

From the perspective of the poor put-upon tabloid readers living under the tyranny of so-called human rights, Jowell is not only getting her just desserts, but a taste of her own medicine to boot... so this quote is probably best understood as delivered with a barely stifled giggle and a missing 'As if!' at the end.

> "It's something that could happen to any of us. I hope the
> council moves fast and gets this sorted out for her."

Becky (24, from London)

28 July 2008

Katie is outraged by "a Facebook virtual knife game" which we are told "encourages kids to stab each other" (i.e. as well as hug and kiss and squeeze and like and 'poke' and so on).

The social-interaction app is available to all ages, but we can let that pass. It has appeared on Facebook, and is not created by Facebook, but that's by the by. The software in question was created by US firm Slide for users of Facebook *and* Myspace, but only Facebook gets a mention, *and* it's further implied that Facebook own/originated it, but don't let it distract you.

Instead, the lady with her boobs out wants you to focus on the stabbing and think about the children:

> "This sick game sends out completely the wrong message.
> Children should be taught that knife crime doesn't pay."

Katie (23, from Liverpool)

Any new trend is an easy target for tabloids, but Facebook was an especially popular target for The Sun, and this almost certainly had nothing to do with Rupert Murdoch investing $580 million in the competing social media interest... Myspace.

Not that relentless character assassination did him any good: Facebook easily overtook Myspace and Murdoch eventually had to settle for a reported selling price of $35 million. [sad trombone]

06 October 2008

Rebekah Wade/Brooks had a personally-held concern for the environment that was out of step with most tabloid folk, but somehow it magically filtered down into the opinion columns of many of her celebrity writers. Not all of them (obviously) but mainly the topless ones, for some reason.

Here, Page 3 favourite Keeley is allegedly "flabbergasted" by news of coffeehouse chain Starbucks wasting 23 million litres of water per day. A report by The Sun calculated that this amount was being poured down the drains of over 10,000 coffeehouses worldwide due to a corporate policy of keeping a tap running all day in every outlet, and Keeley encourages a consumer backlash by predicting one:

> "Everybody knows we should be saving water. Eco-friendly customers may soon be getting their skinny lattes elsewhere."

Keeley (22, from Bromley)

09 December 2008

Still, there are limits to caring about the planet, and on this occasion, Keeley argues that a climate-change demonstration shutting down Stansted airport has backfired:

> "I have some sympathy with protestors, but causing so many planes to divert puts MORE carbon dioxide into the atmosphere."

Keeley (22, from Bromley)

1. The stunt was mainly designed to publicise the issue of cheap flight culture and its contribution to carbon emissions.

2. Any temporary halting of carbon emissions at a single airport was obviously meant to be largely symbolic and only a fool or a scoundrel would argue otherwise.

3. The diversions she mentions are themselves a diversion: fifty scheduled services (to places much further away than the nearest airport) were cancelled outright as a result of the disruption.

06 January 2009

Today, Sam is "gutted" at reports that Morris dancing might be extinct in 20 years:

> "We are losing too many of our traditions. Let's hope Morris men keep waving their hankies for years to come."

Sam (22, from Manchester)

22 January 2009

There are thousands of empty properties in and around London that are owned by wealthy foreigners and locals who use them primarily if not only as investments; the practice keeps precious housing off the market and also creates targets for squatters. Today's topless model Chelsea is reported to be a in state of disbelief about "the cheek" of squatters who have taken hold of two mansions worth an estimated £30million in prestigious Park Lane, London. Obviously her thoughts go out to the honest, working class folk and how angry they should be about this:

> "This is so unfair on all those people who work so
> hard to put a roof over their head."

> *Chelsea (18, from Portsmouth)*

03 February 2009

Ruth is said to be "surprised" to see Britain grinding to a halt in the snow.

Personally, I'm shocked that anyone might be surprised by this, but at least a glamour model is asking the hard questions about it:

> "It was great to see so many people enjoying the
> weather, but why is it our country always struggles to
> cope with snow?"

> *Ruth (25, from Kent)*

13 February 2009

13-year-old Alfie Patten has been named in The Sun as the father of Maisie Roxanne, newborn daughter of 15-year-old Chantelle Steadman. The Sun lead with an image of the lad and baby on the front page next to the headline 'DAD AT 13'. The Conservatives have already seized upon the issue as irrefutable evidence of Britain's social and moral decline, and a tabloid feeding frenzy is about to descend on a series of relatives and associates involving both extended families. Further, young Alfie is about to have his little heart broken in front of the entire country... later DNA results will establish that he is not the father. Obviously, what Alfie needs now more than ever is parenting advice from a topless model in a predatory tabloid.

Today we are told that Poppy is "stunned" to hear that "tiny Alfie" is a dad at just 13, but we are assured that she "admires him sticking by his girlfriend":

> "He is so young to have the burden of fatherhood. And
> he is doing what most lads in his position wouldn't do."

> *Poppy (18, from Somerset)*

20 February 2009

The Sun is running a front page with an image from Google Earth showing grid lines on the ocean floor under the headline 'Is This Atlantis?'

Atlantis experts have been consulted, obviously, but it is not until later when mapping experts become involved that we will find out that this "grid of streets" is in fact a meaningless digital artefact of the sonar data collection process.

Anyway, let's hand over to Ruth, who is reportedly "thrilled" at the idea that "the lost city of Atlantis may have been found":

> "The fabled utopia has captured the imagination of
> scholars for centuries. Plato would be well chuffed if
> he knew about this."
>
> *Ruth (25, from Kent)*

Yes, if the dead could animate, I am certain that Plato would be *very* animated at the idea of a national 'news' paper in the 21st century running a front page story and a topless editorial about the potential discovery of a figment of his imagination.

27 March 2009

The 'Challenge 25' initiative is gaining in popularity among alcohol retailers, including some of the large supermarkets. The policy to ask for ID if the customer looks under 25 (i.e. instead of 18 or 21) is designed to prevent embarrassment by leaving a larger margin for error that also serves as a polite grace for younger customers, but Keeley appears to have missed the point. We are told today that she thinks it's "barmy" that shoppers buying alcohol will be asked for ID if they look under 25, and she has this to say about it:

> "Some people might be flattered, but it could end up
> being embarrassing for others."
>
> *Keeley (22, from Bromley)*

07 May 2009

Marks & Spencer are charging more for larger bras because more fabric. Rhian wants M&S to stop charging £2 extra for bras bigger than DD because reasons:

> "It is terrible that women should be taxed for being
> blessed with big boobs. I'm sure if M&S dropped the tax
> it wouldn't mean going bust."
>
> *Rhian (22, from Manchester)*

12 August 2009

Danni is reportedly "shocked" to hear about "pirates in the English Channel":

> "You hear of pirates in other parts of the world, but you
> never expect them to be in European waters, let alone off
> the English coast. Let's hope it's just a one-off."

Danni (22, from Coventry)

1. A missing Russian-manned cargo ship carrying timber (the MV Arctic Sea) was reported to have been hijacked off the coast of Sweden before disappearing. It was scheduled to later pass through the English Channel, it was not hijacked *in* the channel. 'Pirates may be near the Channel' is already a leap, but suddenly here we are in The Sun with "pirates in the Channel" and "off the English coast."

2. The ship turned up in Cape Verde two weeks later, only to be seized by the Russian Navy... and that was the last anyone in the western world saw or heard of it. So, this was one of two things: a shady deal that the Russian government would rather cover up, something that happens often, or an act of piracy in Northern European waters, something that hasn't happened in centuries.

Foreign & World

05 August 2003

Today we are assured that "Melanie has been keeping track of the civil war in Liberia where government forces and rebels are locked in conflict," and being a gentleman, I am bound to take her at her word. She has this to say about the crisis:

> "I am glad to hear a plane from Britain has arrived in the
> country with badly-needed aid for the thousands of innocent
> people who are the real victims of war. I hope it will not be
> long before things settle down."

Melanie (22, from Watford)

23 December 2003

Michelle is said to be "overjoyed" that British hostage Mark Henderson has been freed in time for Christmas:

> "It's great for his family - they must have been terrified.
> But now they can be reunited."

Michelle (20, from Oldham)

08 May 2007

Nikkala is, as far as we know, "thrilled" at the historic power sharing deal in Northern Ireland and we are almost certain that she had this to say about it:

"No one thought it would ever be possible but this proves peace can always be achieved through democracy. Now Northern Ireland can look forward to a brighter future."

Nikkala (24, from Middlesex)

16 February 2009

Katie is "shocked to learn" that nuclear submarines from the British and French navies have collided. It's not mentioned on this page, but it's no secret that the submarines involved are equipped to fire 16 ballistic missiles carrying up to 48 nuclear warheads. Each.

"This could have been catastrophic. Thank goodness the only thing that was hurt was both countries' seafaring pride."

Katie (23, from Liverpool)

07 June 2007

A tense G8 summit is in progress. Vladimir Putin is upset about a missile shield set up by the US in Poland and the Czech Republic. Bush's administration contends that the shield is aimed at "rogue states" such as Iran, but Putin has spoken of a "hypothetical" situation where he might be forced to point his missiles at Europe.

Blair is positioning himself as the man to bring Russia's strongman leader around with some tough and direct talk, but he leaves office in twenty days and former KGB agent Vladimir Putin has already ignored his formal extradition request for former KGB agent Andrei Lugovoi.

Some think Blair's got high hopes in his weakened state, but not today's topless model. Sam is alleged to be "furious" that Putin has been "stirring up a nuclear threat," and is confident that our beloved PM will give him what for:

"What a nasty piece of work. Thank goodness Tony Blair is going to put him in his place."

Sam (21, from Manchester)

Mr Putin's feelings about any rebuke from a topless model in a British newspaper are not on record, but he humiliated Blair by 'postponing' their scheduled one-to-one meeting at the last minute before forcing Blair to make his pitch on the fringes of the summit, then doing what Putin always does, which is whatever he wants.

05 February 2008

Amylu anticipates "plenty of excitement" about 'Super Tuesday' events determining the final party choices for presidential nominee in the US.

> "It looks like it could be a really close-run contest. And it
> is important, because whatever happens in the US has
> an impact on the rest of the world."
>
> *Amylu (20, from Birmingham)*

Some may sneer at a perceived simplicity or naivety in this example, but I can assure you that topless models do spend time considering world affairs with surprising regularity and in far more detail than you may care to appreciate.

16 June 2008

'Page 3 Idol' winner Jenny is today described as "appalled" at Austria's decision to refuse extradition of a Nazi war criminal on the basis of his advanced years and allegedly poor health. We are advised that new kid on the block Jenny is a university student before we are presented with her alleged opinion on this matter:

> "The Nazis committed crimes against humanity. He
> should be brought to justice no matter how old he is."
>
> *Jenny (18, from the Wirral)*

06 April 2009

Sam is reportedly "concerned to hear that North Korea (has) launched a long-range missile" and offers this:

> "I'm staggered Kim Jong-II is playing such a dangerous
> game despite the ban on testing long-range ballistics."
>
> *Sam (23, from Manchester)*

26 May 2009

Keeley is described as "worried about rogue state North Korea's nuclear ambitions" and we are told that she has this to say:

> "The world will not be a safer place if countries like
> North Korea and Iran are allowed to have these
> dangerous weapons."
>
> *Keeley (22, from Bromley)*

The Economy

Again, I want to make is absolutely clear that it is both cynical and unjust to simply assume that these editorials were decided and dictated mainly if not wholly by deputy editors who were as familiar with their masters' voice as they were with their immediate needs and long-term desires.

Further, I want to make it absolutely clear to any young women reading this book that you are as capable of holding legitimate views on the economy as anyone else... provided that you are sufficiently well-informed, obviously, and not surreptitiously operating according to any unspoken agenda or discreetly veiling an obvious conflict of interest that might undermine the credibility of your argument.

Just saying is all.

26 September 2003

It's three years since the Blair government was badly shaken by nationwide fuel protests. Today, Chancellor of the Exchequer Gordon Brown is under attack from motoring organisations and the Conservatives after agreeing to put up petrol duties by more than 6p a gallon. On Page 3, Michelle "reckons" that fuel prices should be going down instead of up, but takes a stand against recent talk of formal fuel protests anyway:

> "Prices should be in line with other countries. Why should we pay double the amount some people pay? The Government is just being greedy. But I think it would be really bad if there were fuel blockades. It would lead to total chaos."

Michelle (20, from Oldham)

11 December 2003

Melanie is reported to be "outraged" at the idea of council tax bills increasing at four times the rate of inflation in the coming year, but while she may be unimpressed with the "likely 8.2 per cent increase," there are signs that she can be talked around if someone would care to drop by and sort out the bins at her place:

> "I wouldn't mind paying more if I could see some improvement in services. But I've just moved into a new pad and the council hasn't even given me a wheelie bin!"

Melanie (22, from Watford)

08 January 2004

Krystle is apparently convinced that the weak dollar will boost US tourism. So convinced is she by her argument that she speaks openly about potential travel plans:

> "Security worries may have scared some Brits from travelling. But holidays will be cheaper, which may encourage more to book flights. I have family in San Diego and now could be the time to visit."
>
> *Krystle (21, from Manchester)*

Nobody brought security issues up, but clearly it's been weighing on Krystle's mind. Now it's weighing on my mind. Thanks, Krystle.

18 March 2004

Natasha "welcomes" what is described as a "Budget move to sweep away Whitehall waste" and says:

> "I don't want my tax wasted on pen-pushers and bureaucrats. The axe should fall next on those in silly politically-correct council jobs."
>
> *Natasha (21, from Torquay)*

No 'politically correct council jobs' are specified, but sometimes it pays to talk around the so-called minorities and assorted whiners wanting special treatment, as some of them can be real snowflakes about it.

Further, not only is it safer to rubbish any notion of being sensitive to you-know-whatevers generally, but you also play to up to a dozen unspoken prejudices (instead of limiting yourself to one) while simultaneously avoiding risk of specific upset from some bleeding heart liberals who might otherwise fact-check your arse.

26 April 2004

Melanie, like Nikkala, is a streamline reformer and reportedly "furious" about government waste:

> "To think that £20billion of taxpayers' money can be squandered on red tape is horrifying. Our schools and hospitals desperately need that money, not a bunch of bureaucrats. It's got to be tightened up to make sure our taxes reach frontline services."
>
> *Melanie (22, from Watford)*

30 July 2004

Zoe is reported to be upbeat about Britain's reported £1trillion debt. We are told she "thinks nothing of flashing... her credit card" and says:

> "It sounds a lot of money but we are a rich country. As long as you keep your finances in order every month there's nothing wrong with having nice things on credit. If I see a must-have dress I go right out and buy it."

Zoe (22, from London)

25 February 2005

Interesting one, this:

Jak is allegedly "delighted that British business is booming" and we are further assured that "she's doing her own bit for exports - by taking 10,000 advance orders in Japan for her single Come On" *and* has this to say:

> "Profits are up for British business. That's a good sign the economy is doing just fine."

Jak (19, from Tunbridge Wells)

That plug's solid confirmation that the occasional page 3 model has some kind of say about the content of their editorial, but I struggled to find any sign of Jak's progress with this venture and her wider singing career, and so cannot speak with any authority on the practical merits of this product placement and the likely benefit to British business.

23 January 2008

Today, the western world is dealing with the ongoing Financial Crisis of 2007-2008 and news of Heath Ledger's death. It is not a happy time generally, but Mel is "chuffed" to learn of a big cut in US interest rates and says:

> "It's great news. Hopefully, everyone with shares or a pension can breathe a little easier now."

Mel (24, from Morecambe)

Tomorrow, analysts will announce that the US has experienced the largest annual drop in home sales in a quarter of a century. A Great Recession is about to go global, and it will later be determined that the associated US recession had already begun four weeks ago.

12 March 2008

Still, the main concern for the working man is fuel prices, so obviously Jennifer is going to be "delighted" to learn petrol prices will be frozen in today's budget:

> "Finally some good news for drivers! And it's great to see a little relief for families. Rising mortgages and household costs have made life very difficult over the past few months."

Jenny (18, from the Wirral)

28 May 2008

But frozen isn't enough for Keeley, who apparently speaks out today because she "believes petrol prices must come down" and puts it like this:

> "Fat cat bosses of top firms aren't the ones that suffer when petrol is so expensive. I feel sorry for mums on the school run and van drivers who need their vehicles."

Keeley (21, from Bromley)

11 June 2008

It's Wednesday, and we are told that Katie "hopes motorists would not panic-buy petrol when a fuel tanker drivers' strike starts on Friday" and makes the following appeal to the government:

> "That will probably just cause more problems for everyone. The Government needs to do more to help drivers."

Katie (23, from Liverpool)

17 June 2008

The strike by fuel tanker drivers over pay started to hit the domestic supply of petrol and diesel by Saturday, and while the strike ended without a deal on Monday, fuel is still hard to come by on the Tuesday when a Page 3 model is so "shocked" by reports of small-time profiteers including "one filling station owner (who) has put up the price of fuel to £2 a litre" that she just has to speak out:

> "It's outrageous - as if motorists weren't already getting hit in the wallets. The owner may say that he's trying to stop panic buying, but it smacks of pure greed."

Keeley (21, from Bromley)

18 June 2008

Some would prefer to take summer off, but the Financial Crisis of 2007-2008 isn't having any of it, and is busy barreling towards its crisis point barely two months away. Today, we hear Nikkala is "shocked" that local inflation is "heading towards four percent" and we are further advised that she urges consumers to exercise caution:

> "I am definitely curbing my spending. We need to take a deep breath and support each other through these financial tough times."
>
> *Nikkala (24, from Middlesex)*

10 July 2008

Today we are informed that Jenny is "horrified" that the housing crisis has led to "people losing their jobs" and says:

> "It is terrible news for them and their families. I feel so sorry for them. It shows just how tough times are."
>
> *Jenny (18, from the Wirral)*

11 July 2008

But, still, let's stay focused on the issues that impact the average hard-working motorist. Today, Nikkala is purported to be worried about "hard-up families (that) could be hit by... hikes in car tax," saying:

> "Times are hard enough at the moment. This is just another kick in the teeth. I hope the Government has a re-think to give motorists a break."
>
> *Nikkala (24, from Middlesex)*

22 July 2008

Nikkala continues to harbour concerns about motorists being hit in the hip pocket, but today it is reported that she "rushed out to fill her car with petrol last night as prices finally came down," before giving thanks for this silver lining:

> "In these hard times every saving is a help. Let's hope it's the first of many price cuts to come."
>
> *Nikkala (24, from Middlesex)*

05 August 2008

It is a time of harsh economies, so there is no pre-amble on Page 3 today, only Amii's statement*:

> "A break from stamp duty is just what is needed by
> hard pressed homebuyers - and the economy in
> general. Nice one, Gordon!"

Amii (22, from Birmingham)

(*Oh, and a lovely picture of her tits, obviously. Some things are too big to fail.)

03 September 2008

The crisis is deepening and the financial shit is just about to hit the fan, but today we are told that Becky is "delighted that the government has raised the stamp duty threshold," arguing:

> "It should kick-start the housing market and give
> more first-time buyers a chance to get the home of
> their dreams."

Becky (24, from London)

16 September 2008

The shit has hit the fan. Katie is alleged to be "worried by the collapse of the banking giant Lehman Brothers and the meltdown in global financial markets," but reminds us in her own special way that we're all in this together:

> "Everyone seems to be suffering in this credit crunch.
> You just wonder who will be the next to go."

Katie (23, from Liverpool)

26 September 2008

Money both real and imaginary is being madly shuffled around in order to keep crucial aspects of the economy going, but Amy D is specifically "concerned" about "possible knock-on effects" if "George Bush tries to push through a $400bn bail-out for failed US banks" (which would later swell to $700 billion):

> "If the plan falls through it could make the credit
> crunch even worse for us in Britain."

Amy D (20, from Cheshire)

29 September 2008

Today Becky is "disgusted" by reports that "Barclays bankers guzzled champagne in Monte Carlo" while "ordinary Brits struggle with the credit crunch":

> "Everyone else is cutting back, but they're splashing out on a boozy night out."
>
> *Becky (24, from London)*

07 October 2008

There is some debate as to whether this is a crunch or a crash. Amy G seems to think it's a little of both; she is "alarmed by yesterday's FTSE-100 crash" and concludes "the crunch (has) caused yet more financial uncertainty" before saying:

> "These are tough times. Just when you hope it's about to get better it gets worse."
>
> *Amy G (20, from Sheffield)*

09 October 2008

Rhian is reported to be "impressed by Chancellor Alistair Darling's bold plan to rescue our struggling banks". Now, before you say anything, I should point out that even economic experts are allowed to have differing opinions, and that President Bush's plan to bail out banks is entirely distinct from Chancellor Darling's. For starters, the UK 'bank rescue package' involves £500 billion (i.e. $850 billion) which is bigger and therefore better than Bush's mere $700 billion. So there.

> "It's a welcome step forward which hopefully will go some way towards lifting the economic gloom."
>
> *Rhian (21, from Manchester)*

21 October 2008

Today, Katie Leigh allegedly urges readers to "shop local" and back our nation of shopkeepers to "help them beat the credit crunch":

> "Times are tough and we need to support our small businesses to keep them strong through the recession. They are what keeps the country going."
>
> *Katie Leigh (19, from Birmingham)*

07 November 2008

Amy G (not to be confused with fellow topless economy expert Amy D) reportedly claims that an announced 1.5 per cent interest rate cut is "great news for the economy, and homeowners in particular - provided the banks pass it on":

> "It's just what hard-up home-owners need. I really
> hope lenders do the right thing."
>
> *Amy G (20, from Sheffield)*

18 November 2008

Another day when matters are so desperate, there's no time for pre-amble or analysis, only blind optimism and happy thoughts (aka The Tinkerbell Strategy):

> "It's very worrying to hear that we're heading for a
> depression but we'll get through it. Everyone's just
> got to stay positive."
>
> *Keeley (22, from Bromley)*

24 November 2008

Peta is described as "delighted" at news that "the Chancellor intends to slash VAT from 17.5 per cent to 15 per cent" and allegedly says:

> "This is just what we need to help the economy
> through the credit crunch. Every penny counts."
>
> *Peta (22, from Essex)*

26 November 2008

Becky is reported to be "thrilled" about news that Tesco is "slashing the prices of hundreds of products":

> "It's great news - just what everyone needs at a time
> when so many people are struggling. Let's hope it forces
> other supermarkets to reduce their prices as well."
>
> *Becky (25, from London)*

Note: Tesco was not pioneering here, but instead trying to lure lost customers back from other supermarkets with a better reputation for discounts. Four days later, Tesco would announce third-quarter like-for-like sales growth of just 1.9% (down from over 4%), its worst financial performance since the UK Recession of 1991-92.

27 November 2008

Still, let's not concern ourselves with the corporate side of national and global retailing. What really matters is the retail experience for the hardworking customer... and a High St candy crisis on the near horizon! Today, Rhian is said to be "sad that struggling chain Woolworths is to call in the administrators":

> "It's unthinkable Woolies could disappear from the High Street. It's an institution - not least for the pick and mix. I hope a way can be found for it to survive."

Rhian (21, from Manchester)

18 December 2008

But the doom 'n' gloom isn't all about the pick 'n' mix. As the new year approaches, Poppy is further "upset" to hear about "major job losses expected in 2009":

> "Unemployment is already rocketing. Now thousands of Woolworths staff are to lose their jobs. So much for a Happy new year."

Poppy (18, from Somerset)

07 January 2009

Wait, I take that back... it *is* all about the pick 'n' mix! Today we are assured that Rosie is "upset that Woolworths have closed their doors for the last time," because sweets:

> "It's so sad to see an institution like Woolies being driven out of business by the credit crunch. Where will people buy their pick'n'mix now?"

Rosie (18, from Surrey)

29 January 2009

Today, Zoe is said to be "worried" that Britain may be hardest hit in what later turns out to be a global recession:

> "The whole world is going to feel the pinch but it's a hammer-blow to think we'll be worst. I just hope these predictions by the IMF are wrong."

Zoe (27, from London)

06 February 2009

A mere week later, we are told that Becky is "buoyed by the tiny signs of recovery in our gloomy economy":

> "We are not out of the woods yet, but it's great that fat
> cat bankers face bonus curbs, house prices rose in
> January and low interest rates could kickstart spending."

Becky (25, from London)

11 February 2009

In fact, the signs of recovery are so strong that we finally have the luxury of throwing some blame around, and here we are assured that Nikkala says it is "about time former bank bosses said sorry":

> "This was the least they could do after their banks
> failed so spectacularly and sent shock waves
> through our economy."

Nikkala (25, from Middlesex)

18 February 2009

Today, Sam apparently continues with the narrative as she "wholeheartedly backs Gordon Brown's crackdown on the banking bonus culture":

> "These fat cats get paid big enough salaries while
> thousands of hard-working Brits are losing their jobs."

Sam (23, from Manchester)

(At the time of writing, UK bankers are still being paid big salaries with enormous bonuses. A corrected edition of this book will be published if this ever changes.)

24 March 2009

Let's put thoughts of blame aside for a moment. Let's instead keep a weather eye out for those signs of recovery and align ourselves with the cheery optimism of Peta, who is "tickled pink" at reports that "sales of sexy lingerie have soared":

> "Randy Brits are banishing the credit crunch blues by
> buying racy underwear and retreating into the bedroom.
> At last something good to come out of this recession."

Peta (22, from Essex)

03 April 2009

And finally we get back to the subject of those bail-outs. Today we are informed that Rosie says "the G20 leaders did the right thing by injecting a trillion dollars into the world economy" and further singles out the PM for individual praise:

> "It's great to see Gordon Brown pull this off. I'm most
> impressed by his fiscal stimulus package."
>
> *Rosie (18, from Middlesex)*

20 April 2009

Despite the positive opinion some topless models have about Gordon Brown's stimulus package, Katie is reported to be "concerned about Wednesday's budget":

> "I feel for the public sector workers set to lose their jobs.
> And we'll all feel it in the pocket if there are tax hikes to
> cover the Government's borrowing."
>
> *Katie (23, from Liverpool)*

23 April 2009

And today, Keeley allegedly expresses "fears that hard-working, low-earning Brits" will be the main if not only 'victims' of that same Budget:

> "Those battling with their bills will be hit further with tax
> hikes on small luxuries like the odd drink at the local."
>
> *Keeley (22, from Bromley)*

16 July 2009

Soon after, Amii is reportedly "horrified to learn of the record rise in Britain's unemployment figures". In just over a year, unemployment has climbed from roughly 5% to near 8%.

> "It's dreadful. People are having a really rough time. I
> just hope the Government will do everything in its
> power to get us out of this recession."
>
> *Amii (23, from Coventry)*

It is 2009. It will be 2014 before unemployment finally drops below 7% and 2015 before it even approaches 5%, with the latter figures part-supported by mere dreams of pay on 'zero hours' contracts.

20 July 2009

If elected, David Cameron has promised to get tough on bankers and associated City speculators, so today, Sam has "welcomed Conservative plans to crack down on the banks," and she has good reason to be confident, because Tories have a long history of standing up to themselves:

> "Any measures which keep the banks in check have got to be good news. They must be made to behave responsibly."

Sam (23, from Manchester)

06 August 2009

Higher than expected levels of bad debt (over £13.4 billion) beset Lloyds Banking Group, leading to a £4 billion loss in the first half of the year. The government's asset protection scheme covers roughly three-quarters of the loans, with the burden shared between bank shareholders and the taxpayer, and it is on this basis that Rhian (allegedly) assures us that "banking giant Lloyds' plans to dump billions more in toxic debt on the taxpayer" and says:

> "It's a disgrace that the hard-working public is again expected to cover the huge debt racked up by reckless bankers."

Rhian (22, from Manchester)

25 August 2009

But let's not let any of this crisis divert reader attention away from their right to cheap fuel. Today, Becky & Rosie are all smiles but reportedly "furious that the Government is increasing fuel duty by 2p per litre next month":

> "Drivers have been hammered enough... This could spark more protests"

Rosie (18, from Middlesex)

Education

It turns out you *do* need an education, specifically to *avoid* thought control. Now, let's cut straight to the meat, so we can all have our pudding:

22 November 2004

Today we hear of Zoe's support for recent moves to "stamp out school bullying":

> "It breaks my heart that kids are still being bullied in Britain today. There's no excuse for it. Bullies are weak cowards who should be made to realise how cruel they are being. Schools should make a point of being tough on bullies. Childhood should be one of the happiest times of your life."
>
> *Zoe (22, from London)*

Yes, so when a little girl at your local school is missing and quite possibly dead, don't be intimidated into cooperating with any misbehaving tabloid newspaper, especially one owned by Rupert Murdoch and/or edited by Rebekah Wade/Brooks, no matter how much they or their pathetic minions bully you. This message applies equally to both school-aged children, and fully grown adults working as police officers.

27 February 2006

New school discipline measures have Krystle's wholehearted backing, apparently:

> "It's great parents are to be hauled in for detention. Discipline shouldn't just be up to teachers."
>
> *Krystle (23, from Manchester)*

23 February 2009

Sam is reportedly "appalled by our education system", but risks some humour:

> "Labour has turned learning and teaching into a commodity, with their obsession with league tables and progress targets. But we all know the most important lessons are learned behind the bike sheds."
>
> *Sam (24, from Manchester)*

02 April 2009

The final report of the Independent Review of the Primary Curriculum is out, and as you can imagine, everybody is terribly excited about it.

Dubbed the 'Rose Report,' it recommends elevating ICT (Information and Communication Technology) to the same level of importance as the classic Three Rs, reasoning that digital competence is already as important as reading, writing and basic mathematics if you want to get by in life*.

However, today Ruth is reportedly focused on a "sad state of affairs" where "so many kids are going to secondary school without basic English and maths skills," and she's having none of this ICT malarkey:

> "Britain will be in a pretty poor state in a generation
> or two unless something is done."

> *Ruth (25, from Kent)*

(*For the record, I collated these editorials, fact-checked/researched context, typed my snarky remarks and designed every aspect of this book on a home computer using a variety of skills taught in modern ICT.)

The EU

The issue of our membership status in the European Union has become notorious for splitting opinion and causing division, but for some strange and unexplored reason, the Page 3 models were as one voice against the hated EU and their so-called human rights all along. Go figure.

09 October 2003

The Sun has had very little to say about Conservative leader Iain Duncan Smith, and Page 3 even less so. He is easy to ignore because charisma and in any case, The Sun is at this time favouring the Home Office because Blunkett, and acting as the 'Downing Street Echo' because Iraq.

But it's party conference season, IDS is finally getting editorial coverage on Page 3, and today, there is even scant praise for the quiet man, because Europe. Today we are told that Nikkala "applauded" the news of Conservative plans to "fight 'tooth and nail' against the new EU constitution" before saying this:

> "Labour is letting the country drift into the hands of Europe. The Tories have now stood up and said they aren't going to accept this. It shows Iain Duncan Smith has some backbone and could save him as leader. But I think the party has to do a lot more before they can even think about winning the next General Election."
>
> *Nikkala (21, from Middlesex)*

Soon after, Nicola T would dismiss him as "boring" and it would all be over (see Page 79), but for one glorious moment in October 2003, Iain Duncan Smith was mildly approved of by a topless model because of his willingness to free us from the jackboot of EU oppression.

12 December 2003

Today, Michelle is reported to be "furious at the prospect of Brussels bureaucrats playing havoc with our establishment" and it is further alleged that she says this of the new European Constitution:

> "This is like an invasion through the back door. These people want to take control of our borders, our courts and even our oil and gas. Generations of soldiers have died while protecting our freedom and now they're going to shackle us without a fight."
>
> *Michelle (20, from Oldham)*

21 April 2004

The Sun and Page 3 are taking a rare stand against Tony Blair, seeking to convince him to shun the proposed EU Constitution (aka the Constitutional Treaty).

Yesterday, Blair made a significant u-turn on the Constitutional Treaty and offered the nation a referendum on the subject... but that's clearly not enough for The Sun, who have conducted their own 'hotline' poll of readers in response, because they're in a hurry to free themselves from tyranny.

Today, we are told that Charlotte expects Tony Blair to be "stunned" by the results of their poll, and had this to say about it:

> "The PM will choke on his cornflakes when he reads how many Sun readers don't want him to sign up to the constitution. In his heart of hearts, he knows they represent the country."
>
> *Charlotte (19, from Ipswich)*

To his credit, Blair declined this invitation to accept the overnight 'hotline' poll from a single tabloid newspaper as binding, and continued to offer a referendum. To allay fears/criticisms of stalling, he put a promise of a referendum on the Constitutional Treaty in Labour's 2005 election manifesto.

31 May 2005

Blair's decision to allow a referendum has led to other EU countries offering the same, only their leaders have been far quicker about it. Spain said 'Sí' earlier in the year, and France have just said 'Non'. Many protectors of freedom at The Sun are delighted about the latter result, as you might expect, and today's topless model is no exception. Becky is reported to be "delighted" with the result and alleged to be the author of this charming backhander:

> "It's not often the French are our friends, but they have done us proud."
>
> *Becky (24, from London)*

The French public had rejected the Constitution by a margin of 55% to 45% on a turnout of 69%. A few days later, the Dutch rejected the Constitution by a margin of 61% to 39% on a turnout of 62%. The earlier positive vote from Spanish voters (76% voting in favour to 24% against) on a turnout of 43% was looking distinctly overshadowed, with only a further positive vote from little Luxembourg to follow.

Ratification of the Constitutional Treaty stalled at this point, and all other scheduled referendums were cancelled soon after. On 6 June 2005, Jack Straw announced that the government's plans for a referendum had been shelved. However, The Sun was not to be silenced: the UK had to have its chance to say 'no'.

03 July 2005

Today, we are informed that Louise thinks we here in the UK "should be given the chance to reject the hated EU treaty" and we are further assured that she has this to say about the matter:

> "Tony Blair promised us a referendum. Most Brits would jump at the chance to go to the polls and say No."

> *Louise (19, from Manchester)*

What The Sun really recommends here is that we as a nation undergo a full and robust campaign and an expensive national referendum just for the sake of telling a few foreigners to piss off, because what Louise fails to mention about the "hated" Constitutional Treaty is that it was so disliked that it had already been told to go away and become a nothing.

Leaders of EU countries took a long time to come back with a solution to this rejection of the new Constitutional Treaty, and it was in the form of a series of amendments to existing treaties (primarily the Treaty of Rome and the Treaty of Maastricht). Ultimately known as the Lisbon Treaty, it was agreed in October 2007 and signed in December 2007.

All of this happened very slowly and very deliberately to avoid any constitutional issues, but none of that mattered to certain parties who had been promised a referendum on a treaty that no longer existed over changes that were no longer being sought.

Even after Blair left and Brown took charge, The Sun sought to hold Brown to Blair's promise, refusing to acknowledge any difference between the Constitutional Treaty and the reforms proposed in the wake of its rejection, because manifesto promises overrule manifest reality. Oh, and they were still using reader polls in a bold attempt to decide the matter for us...

27 September 2007

Today, Keeley is reportedly "delighted so many Sun readers backed an EU referendum" and allegedly says:

> "Britain has spoken. Now Gordon Brown must show he's a man of his word and let us vote."

> *Keeley (21, from Bromley)*

Later, Brexit happened. The end.

The Expenses Scandal

It is March 2008. The credit crunch and the banking bailouts have dominated the previous year and the world is headed for a global recession in the worst financial crisis since the Great Depression.

Meanwhile, Sir Peter Viggers (Conservative MP for Gosport) is into his third year of claiming tens of thousands of pounds in expenses for upkeep of a second home he is about to sell for £800K, and the people who bear that expense have no idea... yet.

In the space of those same three years, campaigners and reporters have been pursuing FOI requests for details of MPs expenses claims, with Parliament fighting them every step of the way. By now this battle has just swung firmly against Commons authorities, with the Information Commissioner making their first rulings for specific disclosures... but MPs are increasingly concerned about how their individual and/or collective liberties with expenses are going to play in the current economic climate, and they are just about to experience a taste of public anger upon release of the notorious 'John Lewis' list.

Corruption is about to deepen out of fear of retribution, and the Parliamentary Expenses Scandal is about to peak and then explode into the public arena as a result. The House of Commons has failed to prevent the disclosure of expenses data, and authorities are about to switch to a desperate new plan to censor it; it is the latter effort that will lead directly to their undoing.

14 March 2008

Today we are assured that Vikki "can't believe" that MPs are permitted to "spend thousands of pounds of taxpayers' cash in John Lewis" and says:

> "Politicians should be pumping this money into our schools and hospitals, not their front rooms. It's outrageous."
>
> *Vikki (18, from Essex)*

The 'John Lewis List' was used by officials in the House of Commons to determine if individual expenses claims (e.g. for a flat screen TV) were within reasonable cost.

It was called the 'John Lewis List' because it was based on the prices of likely expenses-covered items at John Lewis stores; this figure was used to calculate a reasonable maximum amount for everything from dishwashers to dining room tables. It was *not* called the 'John Lewis List' because the MPs were all shopping at John Lewis, because they weren't.

I am certain that Vikki regrets any confusion. Moving on...

26 March 2008

Parliament is actively working to prevent disclosure involving a mere 14 MPs. Instead of meeting the deadline of a disclosure ruling by the Information Tribunal, the House of Commons has appealed against the ruling in a last ditch attempt to keep big, juicy chunks of incriminating data under the rug* where they belong. It is in this context that we are informed that Danni is "furious" with MPs:

> "I can't believe they're using taxpayer's cash to go to court to stop us knowing what they spent our money on. It's outrageous. I hope they lose - it will serve them right."

> *Danni (21, from Coventry)*

(*Trivia: the maximum amount an MP could claim for a rug was £300. Each.)

There was even a later attempt to change the law so FOI requests did not apply to MPs expenses going forward, but by January 2009, House of Commons authorities announced that full disclosure of all MPs' expenses would be published on 1 July 2009. By this time, their back-up plan was to redact like hell for reasons of 'privacy', but an unredacted copy of every expenses claim by every MP over a four year period would soon be released as a direct result of Parliament's attempts to censor this same data. Responding to subsequent queries about specific source(s) within the redaction process at the time, whistleblower John Wick had this to say:

> *"What was interesting was the anger that was felt by all the people involved in the redaction process to what they were seeing and the way in which the House of Commons authorities were trying to cover up. The team carrying out the censorship was made up of civil servants, private contractors and of course the moonlighting soldiers. It covered a complete cross section of all ages, backgrounds, race and religion and they all felt the rage at what they were seeing." - **John Wick, Sep 2009**

John Wick approached several national newspapers with the data in March 2009.

31 March 2009

Earlier this week, The Times made a decision to not pay John Wick for the raw expenses data, and instead ran a story about their being offered the data by "a businessman". The Sun have also been approached, but today they choose to play coy by merely referencing an item about an earlier disclosure: the amount that the typical MP can claim in expenses (up to £23K a year). Subsequently, Poppy is said to be "disgusted at how much of our cash MPs are claiming on their expenses":

> "I can't believe hard-working taxpayers' money is going to furnish their homes. It's not as though MPs are hard up, is it?"

> *Poppy (18, from Somerset)*

In the book 'No Expenses Spared' (Robert Winnett, Gordon Rayner) it is reported that high-ups from The Sun were in talks with John Wick at this time, but "wanted to cherry-pick the expenses claims of the most high-profile MPs, and leave the vast majority untouched."

However, Wick held firm on his 'all or nothing' position, and this was how The Sun denied themselves access to the data that was later so assiduously and doggedly followed up by the Telegraph. Their political/tabloid agenda got in the way, and they simply did not understand that Wick could not and would not betray the public with a further cover-up.

Also, I doubt they did themselves any favours by trying to capitalise on privileged knowledge of the data before arriving at any formal agreement with Wick.

07 April 2009

Today, Rhian is reportedly "amazed that so many ministers are embroiled in the expenses scandal," and we are assured that she has this to say about a specific Labour minister:

> "I can't understand why Margaret Beckett didn't live in her caravan. It would have been cheaper for everyone."

> *Rhian (22, from Manchester)*

17 April 2009

Today we are assured that Rhian thinks the "curtain is coming down" on another Labour minister's career. The Home Secretary certainly faces embarrassment over the decision by the CPS not to prosecute Conservative MP Damian Green or the Home Office civil servant who leaked data to him, but it's hard to see how a previous expenses embarrassment has any bearing on any of this unless you're fingering a goldmine of further expenses data and just can't help referencing it.

> "The second home allowance and her husband's porn on expenses were bad enough. But Damian Green being cleared over Home Office leaks could be the final nail in her coffin."

> *Rhian (23, from Manchester)*

The Sun were denied a deal soon after, and on 29 April the Telegraph sent their final contract to Wick. The first disclosures would begin in the pages of the Telegraph newspaper on 8 May 2009.

The Sun, denied the opportunity to direct public anger according to their agenda through selective disclosure, could only play keep-up.

19 May 2009

The Parliamentary Expenses Scandal has hit Westminster like a tornado of shit sandwiches and parties of all colours are having to take multiple bites after a series of devastating disclosures in the Telegraph.

By now it is quite evident what MPs were trying to cover up (and why), the Speaker has been under pressure to resign for a week, and things are coming to a head in the House. It is time for a topless model to speak up for the common man.

Today we are assured that "Katie wants Commons Speaker Michael Martin to stand down," and offers the following statement to support her contention:

> "It's too late for apologies over MPs' expenses. He should listen to politicians and members of the public who demand he goes."
>
> *Katie (23, from Liverpool)*

Later that day, Martin announced plans to stand down. It is unknown what bearing if any Page 3 had on his decision.

19 June 2009

Speaker Martin made his last appearance as Speaker earlier this week, and the day after, MPs' expenses claims were finally published by the House of Commons... with many details redacted. Today, Amii is allegedly "appalled" at what she describes as "the latest attempt to cover up the expenses of MPs":

> "Party leaders constantly speak of the need for transparency on claims but once again we've been kept in the dark. It just shows our MPs are horribly out of touch."
>
> *Amii (23, from Birmingham)*

As justified as this position may seem, any perceived moral authority of The Sun is undermined by attempts to select and direct revelations for political purposes rather than embrace any true principle of transparency.

Further, The Sun did no active investigating of MPs' expenses that bears mentioning: they mainly if not only played keep-up and ran with front pages based on somebody else's hard work, because even when the data was set to fall into their laps, their tabloid agenda got in the way. Worse, The Sun and their alumni now answer criticism of the same tabloid agenda by citing the expenses scandal as an example of the kind of thing that would not happen without their allegedly high standards of investigative journalism.

The truth is The Sun did very little on expenses that could be described as their own work... though their efforts to capitalise on the Parliamentary expenses scandal through angry editorials on Page 3 were unquestionably original.

Health

This sample of editorials suggests that the tabloid version of a 'good health' plan involves not drinking too much, not eating too much, avoiding unprotected sex and illegal drugs... and staying out of the sun.

By sheer coincidence, many celebrities use this same list to stay out of The Sun.

04 May 2005

Keeley is reportedly "concerned" to hear of a new home-testing kit capable of detecting a baby's sex early in pregnancy, and foresees a problem:

> "This could mean a big rise in abortions. It's not something we should encourage."

Keeley (20, from Bromley)

27 May 2004

Charlotte is described as "horrified" by the levels of obesity among British children, and blames the parents:

> "It is shocking. It is the parents' responsibility to make sure their kids eat a balanced diet. Parents need to put away the crisps, biscuits and sugary drinks and make sure children eat more fresh fruit and vegetables."

Charlotte (19, from Ipswich)

20 January 2005

It has been reported that one million admissions to UK emergency department units each year are alcohol-related, with ambulance services especially stretched on Friday and Saturday nights. Today, we are assured that Krystle is "against binge drinking" and "backs calls for pubs to stop selling cheap booze". Not that she's being a killjoy...

> "We all like a good time but the Government is right to take the lead."

Krystle (21, from Manchester)

23 July 2008

But the good times keep rolling, and years later, the UK is left with exactly the same problem. However, this time, the topless model on Page 3 is described as "sad" that the Government has had to once again "threaten action curbing excess boozing" as she attempts to reason with binge-drinking readers:

> "Ignoring warnings over safe levels of drinking causes huge health, financial and anti-social problems."
>
> *Sam (22, from Manchester)*

26 August 2008

Parents can't do it alone, even with Page 3 on their side, so when Danni becomes "alarmed at the youth health crisis," she attempts to reason with celebrity readers:

> "Parents and teachers need to warn youngsters of the dangers of booze, drugs and unprotected sex - but we also need more positive role models."
>
> *Danni (21, from Coventry)*

28 April 2009

The 2009 flu pandemic is unfolding and the first two cases in Scotland have just been reported. Amii urges us "not to panic over swine flu," as she attempts to reason with all British readers:

> "It has led up to 149 deaths in Mexico, but thankfully none here. If it becomes a pandemic we should be in a strong position to cope."
>
> *Amii (23, from Birmingham)*

11 May 2009

The influenza pandemic has gone global. There are already near to a hundred confirmed cases in the UK, and those numbers are about to get a lot bigger. Globally, swine flu will take over 14,000 lives, but today, Amii "cannot believe that so many women are risking their lives for the sake of a sun tan" and says:

> "Your health must come first. It's not worth putting your life in danger just because you want a healthy glow."
>
> *Amii (23, from Birmingham)*

Immigration

There's nothing racist about talking about immigration, and there's nothing bigoted about being angry or afraid of all the things one naturally associates with immigrants... like the word 'illegal', for example. Oh, and 'floods'.

Further, there's clearly a problem with immigrants, because we keep reading about it in the tabloids. They're always coming over here, not speaking our language and scrounging our benefits and taking our jobs. Apparently.

07 February 2005

Today we are introduced to 'stunning' Nicola T, and we are assured that she "backs Labour's tough stance on immigration. Well, as long as those in real need are not targeted," obviously. We're not monsters.

> "We must be sure people in need of genuine help are
> not turned away. That would go against everything
> Britain stands for."

Nicola T (22, from London)

26 April 2006

Ami is reportedly "outraged" at the number of "foreign criminals" who have been "left to roam the streets instead of being deported" in her view:

> "It really is a shocking state of affairs. Sun readers will be
> absolutely furious. How can you possibly feel safe?"

Ami (19, from Birmingham)

28 July 2006

Nikkala is described as both "stunning" and "horrified by the latest immigration scandal," after The Sun exposes an alleged 'cash for asylum' racket:

> "It is disgusting that these crooks are being allowed to
> manipulate the system. Home Secretary John Reid has
> got to act quickly on The Sun's damning dossier."

Nikkala (24, from Middlesex)

23 August 2006

The Home Office has revealed that - over a two year period - 447,000 people from new EU states have successfully applied to work in the UK. Home Office minister Tony McNulty further noted that the figure would be nearer 600,000 if self-employed workers (e.g. builders) were included. Now watch that number magically turn into (near to) a million:

Today, Britain's budding rose Keeley is reportedly "shocked to learn so many immigrants have come to the UK" and says:

> "To think around a million have rushed here in
> two years is staggering. And while most are here
> to work hard for a better life we can't have an
> open door to everyone."

> *Keeley (19, from Bromley)*

17 July 2008

Katie is allegedly "stunned that illegal immigrants smuggled themselves into Britain from Kosovo on board Army lorries" and says:

> "They were only discovered once they got into the
> Army base, which is a shocking security lapse."

> *Katie (23, from Liverpool)*

The group of ~~illegal immigrants~~ asylum seekers included three Indians aged 18-26, a 16-year-old Afghan and a 15-year-old Iranian. The 'Army lorries' were low-loaders driven by civilian contractors carrying military Land Rovers, and while the convoy was travelling from Kosovo, the stowaways boarded when it stopped in Calais. They were also caught within minutes of arriving at the base as part of the usual entry-vetting procedure. But who knows what they might have achieved had they had the opportunity, and perhaps a plan. Some training, maybe. Weapons, even.

18 March 2009

Amii allegedly thinks it's "a worrying state of affairs that so many schoolchildren in Britain don't speak English as their first language" and says:

> "It must affect their learning - and that of those
> around them."

> *Amii (22, from Birmingham)*

So please think of the children. Well, less about the foreign ones, obviously; we have to be practical.

Iraq and 'The War on Terror'

1. This is a long chapter, because Page 3 editorials mentioned war a lot. Quite a lot, actually. This may have had something to do with the Sun's much-heralded role as a fundraising champion for the military, it may equally have been due to Page 3's known presence in footlockers and portaloos on the front lines. Or coincidence.

2. It was a false argument that Iraq and the terrorism threat were related that ultimately led to them *being* related. By invading another country without due cause or an exit strategy, we gave terrorists the outrage, chaos and opportunity their tactics can and did thrive on. However, the entire disaster was dominated by the 'war on terror' narrative (be it stated or implied) and it tainted every debate you could imagine about war, domestic security, intelligence, free speech, and what we were supposed to call 'French Fries', so here we are.

3. All of the following editorial samples begin roughly five months after the March 2003 invasion of Iraq, at a time when serious questions were already being asked about Downing Street's case for war, based as it was upon claims of WMDs that had yet to be found. Everything from angry rhetoric to religious extremism is feeding on outrage after outrage both locally and abroad, and 'Our Boys' have been led into war with an army as ill-equipped as Tony Blair's argument, which will be under constant assault until the day he resigns.

Iraq

15 August 2003

Today we are assured that Nicola T "has been following the Hutton Inquiry into the death of government scientist David Kelly" and has this verdict to share:

> "The only clear thing about the inquiry is that someone is lying. Whether it's politicians or the BBC, it is very worrying. I just hope we get to the bottom of it soon and find out the truth."

Nicola T (21, from London)

Regrettably, Nicola T presented her worrying dichotomy only days into an inquiry that months later failed to arrive at one of these two answers by determining that things were a bit more complex than that: Andrew Gilligan could not substantiate what he asserted the government "probably knew," because there was no way of being sure exactly what the government knew, or the extent to which they had sought to mislead the public. However, while the ruling made clear there was no evidence of a lie by the government, it left room for a shedload of exaggeration.

16 December 2003

It is almost 9 months since the invasion of Iraq. The military occupation has been such a bloody and unexpected disaster that the Bush administration is struggling to portray it in a positive light, but the capture of Saddam Hussein is a rare success story that allows politicians and their supporting media to remind people why we invaded Iraq in the first place: because Saddam ~~had WMDS and was a threat~~ was a terrible person.

> "It was the news we have all waited for. That terrible man tried to crush the Iraqi people. Now they can celebrate their freedom and rebuild their country. I really hope this is the beginning of the end of the troubles in Iraq."
>
> *Krystle (20, from Manchester)*

03 February 2004

Easily my favourite Page 3 editorial. Today we are assured that "Zoe is certain Tony Blair was right to take Britain into war with Iraq" and further informed that she offers this reasoning in support of her/Blair's straw-man argument:

> "You don't have to be an international diplomat to realise the world is better off without Saddam. We should be proud of what has been achieved."
>
> *Zoe (22, from London)*

At this point in time, according to Iraq Body Count, an estimated 10,000 Iraqi civilians have died from conflict since the invasion.

Iraq Body Count started counting civilian deaths because the US administration leading the invasion said it didn't do body counts. In six years of conflict in Iraq, Iraq Body Count determined that there were over 100,000 civilian deaths from related violence. A later data leak revealed that the US government *had* been counting, but the available figures didn't start until nine months after the invasion for some reason: they counted 66,081 civilian deaths from January 2004 to December 2009.

26 February 2004

But do keep in mind that it's all about Saddam, and what a bad person he is. Today, Melanie is "full of pride after 96 Gulf War II heroes received their medals" and says:

> "Their exploits were an inspiration. They deserve all the praise they get after going beyond the call of duty to topple Saddam."
>
> *Melanie (23, from Watford)*

07 April 2004

Dick Cheney predicted that the people of Iraq would welcome US troops as liberators. They didn't. An armed insurgency began in Iraq soon after the invasion.

At this point in time, the US-led multinational force and elements of the post-2003 Iraqi government are both targeted by a range of militants and militias, but it will be a couple of years before the situation deteriorates into a sectarian civil war. There have also been unconnected terrorist attacks in Iraq, primarily suicide bombings killing many more civilians than military.

However, we are told that Natasha "believes it's vital our troops remain in Iraq" and the predominate/official narrative involves the US and partners invading Iraq and then 'staying the course' in order to fight religious extremism and prevent terrorism. That is why today everybody in the insurgency is classified as an 'extremist' by a topless model from Torquay:

> "Our Boys are doing a fantastic job peacekeeping. To give in to a minority of extremists would be an insult to the brave soldiers who lost their lives fighting to free Iraq from its evil regime."
>
> *Natasha (21, from Torquay)*

02 July 2004

Ruth allegedly hails Saddam Hussein's recent court appearance as "a triumph for Iraqis" but in typical tabloid fashion thinks that hanging's too good for him.

> "This was a great moment for the people of Iraq. Yet many will feel that a proper trial seems too good for a man who denied the same right to millions of victims."
>
> *Ruthie (22, from Kent)*

10 December 2004

Bush has been elected for a second term. Iraq is a bloodbath, the world now knows about Abu Ghraib, serious questions are being asked about torture, *and* there are growing calls for an inquiry into civilian deaths. It is at this point that Nicola T reminds us that "people are too keen to forget the help given to Britain by the US" and says:

> "People are too quick to condemn America. We're indebted to them for the help they gave us in the war. Imagine if they had decided not to support us."
>
> *Nicola T (22, from London)*

19 January 2005

The Sun made very little mention of the Abu Ghraib scandal 9 months ago. When news first broke, they relegated it to Page 6 with a mere 130 words and a single image. No editorial. No outrage. The next day, there were only 229 words (not including the editorial headlined 'Bad Apples'). The day after that, Piers Morgan published the fake photos of abuse that should have finished his media career, and *bang*, The Sun had a front page headline and a multi-page spread featuring every image with a whopping 929 words on the subject of fake images of detainees being abused. Priorities, y'see.

However, The Sun do take a mildly stronger line when confronted with evidence of 'Our Boys' engaging in abuse of detainees, which is why today we are told that Ruthie is "angered by photos of British troops abusing Iraqi prisoners" and says:

> "Stories like these play right into the hands of our enemies. People who abuse prisoners must be punished."
>
> *Ruthie (23, from Kent)*

20 October 2005

But have we mentioned recently that it's all about Saddam, and what a bad person he is?

Today, Nicola T is described as "pleased to see Saddam Hussein finally go on trial yesterday - despite his stalling tactics" and says:

> "A lot of people in Iraq have been waiting for this for a long time. Once the trial resumes they will want to see justice being done."
>
> *Nicola T (22, from London)*

Domestic Islamic Extremism

22 January 2004

Ruth is described as being "desperate" to witness Abu Hamza "kicked out of Britain" and The Sun is claiming to have poll results showing that 98.4% of people agree with her:

> "I'm not at all surprised that The Sun has been swamped with support for its campaign."
>
> *Ruth (23, from Bolton)*

This 'poll data' was from an overnight hotline that got a response from about 1% of their readership (using The Sun's own readership figures), but made roughly 3.5K for The Sun and BT in the process. In other words, a mere 1% of Sun readers cared enough about Abu Hamza to spend 10p on contributing to the relevant 'poll'. This was a common device from The Sun at the time, and they would often claim to have support from over 90% of readers, when in fact they had only received a clear vote of support from a tiny percentage of readers with sufficient will and phone credit.

28 May 2004

On 27 May 2004, British citizen Abu Hamza was detained on remand by local authorities and appeared before magistrates at the start of a process to try to extradite him to the United States. Yemen were also requesting his extradition. Today, topless model Michelle is quoted on Page 3 as being glad that the "hate-filled cleric" would be "slinging his hook" and says:

> "Send him to America to face the consequences of
> what he's done. He hates Britain and is bad news.
> We're better off without him."

> *Michelle (21, from Oldham)*

21 December 2004

Abu Hamza has been claiming legal aid for his fight against allegations of incitement to murder and intent to stir up racial hatred . These and wider benefits received by Hamza and his family are seen as excessive by some. In support of this view, Zoe apparently declares that "Hamza should not be getting any handouts" and says:

> "He has some nerve threatening legal action. Here's a
> man who is accused of some very serious crimes. There
> would be public uproar if he got any more cash."

> *Zoe (23, from London)*

18 January 2005

Today Keeley is allegedly "staggered" at the idea of Muslim cleric Omar Bakri Mohammed "(getting) away with his sick rants" and says:

> "I find it amazing that he has been allowed to stay
> this long. Why the Government have put up with him
> and his vile views is beyond me."

> *Keeley (18, from Bromley)*

14 March 2005

Just to show it's nothing personal, today we are told that Katie "reckons Julia Heaton must be mad to marry Abu Hamza" and says:

> "Nobody should be that desperate. Abu is an ugly fanatic. Julia should find someone else. There are plenty of fish in the sea."
>
> *Katie (19, from Liverpool)*

20 July 2005

Nicola T is reportedly "furious" over Omar Bakri and his "latest rants against Britain" and has this to say:

> "He claims thousands in benefits but still sees fit to attack the very people who have supported him. He is a disgrace."
>
> *Nicola T (22, from London)*

In 2006, a British court found Abu Hamza guilty of inciting violence. He was later extradited to the US, found guilty of eleven terrorism charges by a federal jury, and sentenced to life in prison with no possibility of parole. In 2014, a Lebanese court sentenced Omar Bakri to six years for association with the Nusra Front.

For the record, I do not care for religious extremists who prey on the hate and fear of weak-minded mobs with no care for the human cost... but I have similar issues with tabloids. Religious extremists present a challenge to any healthy democracy, but focusing on one religion over the other in constant search of a bogeyman to furnish your 'we invaded Iraq to avoid terror at home' narrative is equally damaging to the foundations of that same democracy. It's also worth asking where David Blunkett stood on these media attacks on targets of the Home Office (see Page 82).

Domestic Security

19 July 2004

A secret dossier containing counter-terrorism plans for Heathrow airport has been found "flapping at the roadside" outside a nearby petrol station and handed to The Sun newspaper. Today, Nicola T is "horrified" at the security breach and says:

> "You would have thought that with the current terrorist threat airports would be the most secure places. It is shocking that this could happen. Security needs tightening as soon as possible."
>
> *Nicola T (21, from London)*

27 July 2004

Today, Anna is alleged to be "shocked" that the government has "taken so long to release its (Preparing for Emergencies) leaflet".

The widely-mocked Preparing for Emergencies initiative is also facing serious criticism from those who think this public information scheme sails too close to an ongoing narrative of war-justifying terror threats being pushed by the same government.

Yes, the 12-page booklet (with supporting website) does cover a range of specific emergency types, but these range from fires and explosions to bombs and chemical, biological or radiological 'incidents', lending a certain flavour to the mix. It also devotes two whole pages to the subject of terrorism, including a concluding page promoting the many and often secret preventative measures being taken by the government to protect the innocent from terrorist attack.

Blair is very sensitive about any talk of scaremongering, which is why it's so amusing that today's topless model comes right out and calls it a "'terror attack' leaflet" before directly associating it with "9/11":

> "Why has it taken so long to bring out a 22-page pamphlet on basic planning for emergencies like keeping a supply of batteries, food and water? This should have been rushed out after 9/11."
>
> *Anna (22, from London)*

24 August 2004

A new sport of 'proving' how easy it would be for a terrorist to blow up this or that has begun among tabloids. Basically, self-described reporters looking to make a name for themselves try all sorts of tricks to smuggle themselves into secure areas with fake bombs and then publish their success stories. Fashionable targets include Parliament, airports, and military bases.

In this instance, a Sun reporter has secured employment with a contractor at Birmingham Airport before smuggling a 200g 'bomb' (made of plasticine, a timer, batteries and wire) past the metal detectors, using his steel-capped boots as cover.

Today, Krystal is reportedly "disgusted" at "lax security that let a Sun reporter smuggle a fake bomb on to a plane" and says:

> "With the massive terror threat hanging over this country, it is incredible that this could happen."
>
> *Krystle (21, from Manchester)*

16 June 2005

On this occasion, our brave Sun reporter has posed as "warfare student" to make an appointment at the Central Library of the Royal Military Academy at Sandhurst, before wandering off into cadet accommodation blocks and back to his car to build a pretend bomb out of plasticine and bits from Maplins. The combination of these two events has led The Sun to claim in a front page splash headline that their reporter "could have blown (Prince) Harry to bits" and Page 3 favourite Zoe apparently has this to say about it all:

> "Why are the Royals so poorly protected? I'm appalled that a Sun reporter managed to walk around unchallenged. He could have been a terrorist. Lessons need to be learned before it is too late."
>
> *Zoe (24, from London)*

29 June 2005

Labour's 2005 election manifesto pledged that - if elected - they would "introduce ID cards... backed up by a national register, and rolling out initially on a voluntary basis as people renew their passports".

At present, many people are concerned about the relevant database and/or how much weight the word 'initially' is carrying, but today in The Sun we are told that Neval is mainly concerned about expense to the (initially) voluntary user, "believes putting a cap on the cost of an ID card is vital", and warns:

> "It's a good idea - but £100 is still expensive. If they help protect British citizens, then fine. But the Government need to make sure these cards are going to be worth the money."
>
> *Neval (22, from London)*

03 August 2005

Nikkala is allegedly "appalled" at the idea that "MPs are swanning off on holiday while fanatics plot against Britain and thugs terrorise the streets" and warns:

> "Everyone needs a break but 80 days is daft. The police are overrun. They desperately need new laws to help them. MPs should cut short their hols before it's too late."
>
> *Nikkala (23, from Middlesex)*

I've almost run out of words on this page. You'll want to turn to the next page, before it's too late.

24 August 2005

Ruth is reportedly "horrified to learn that our borders are so poorly regulated - with thousands entering without even an interview" and says:

"In the current climate it's ludicrous."

Ruth (22, from Kent)

By sheer coincidence, today is the day that Tony Blair will outline new security measures, including fast-tracking of proposed improvements to border controls.

09 November 2005

Both Blair and Wade/Brooks are banking heavily on a proposal to allow police to detain terrorist suspects without charge for up to 90 days. Even Page 3 is all-in to the extent of actively lobbying readers to call the latest hotline 'poll' *and* vote a certain way. Today we are told that "Krystle backs The Sun campaign to see the new terror laws pushed through" and says:

"It is so important the police are given the power they need to combat terrorism. Every reader must lend their weight to this vital campaign and call our hotline."

Krystle (23, from Manchester)

Even if we put this and other result-rigging behaviour to one side, when calling to 'vote' costs 10p, you're really not going to hear from a lot of undecideds. After much scaremongering, The Sun convinced roughly 100,000 readers to call in and say 'yes' to 90 days: just under 3% of readers thought it important to do so.

None of this stopped The Sun from later claiming that 97% of readers supported Blair's 90-day detention plan. An editorial even bragged about the 'thousands more' who had lobbied MPs online in "near-record numbers". This followed The Sun's publication of a list of 257 email addresses of MPs that they wanted readers to target. I used this list myself: not all of the addresses worked, and after making contact with a series of MPs and staff about the volume of email they received as a result of The Sun's campaign, I calculated that no more than 1,500 readers had bothered to email an MP from a working list of approx 232 addresses, with some MPs receiving maybe one and others no more than four negative emails as a result.

Blair lost the '90 days' vote, and it cost him significantly. The next morning, Wade/Brooks ran with a front page and editorial raging against the "traitors" who voted against Blair. Her certainty about the significance of her poll is quite evident:

"TREACHEROUS MPs betrayed the British people last night by rejecting new laws to combat terror. They IGNORED the wishes of the vast majority of Britons and HUMILIATED Tony Blair by inflicting his first Commons defeat."

29 January 2007

Keeley apparently has "mixed feelings" about "anti-terror X-ray machines which can see through clothes" and says:

> "I'm for it - I've got nothing to hide. But some will
> see it as yet more intrusion."

Keeley (20, from Bromley)

For the record, the "nothing to hide" argument generally is bullshit, and in this instance it comes to us from someone who famously had a 'sex tape' suppressed by The Sun and then-editor Rebekah Wade/Brooks.

12 June 2008

Almost three years ago, Blair pressed for 90-day detention without trial for terrorism suspects, but got smacked down to 28 days. Now Brown is in charge, and the government is asking for 42 days... but The Sun are a long way from all-in this time, and Page 3 is no exception. Today's topless model Claire allegedly thinks that "the 42-days detention measure means the authorities will have to strike a delicate balance between preserving civil liberties and protecting the British public from terrorists" and further says:

> "(It shouldn't be used) without strong and valid reasons".

Claire Tully (24, from Dublin)

Brown only just avoided a humiliating defeat in the House of Commons, scraping though with a 9-vote margin, but later had to abandon the plan for 42-day detention when it was defeated by 191 votes in the House of Lords.

30 September 2008

Yesterday it was announced that an unnamed Cabinet Office official would be charged under the Official Secrets Act after leaving top-secret documents on a Surrey train. This followed an earlier theft of an MoD laptop from a McDonalds. Today it appears that a camera sold on eBay for £17 contained secret documents stored in the camera's memory card, including "MI6 documents relating to an operation against al-Qaeda insurgents in Iraq," according to an 'expert' quoted by The Sun. Rosie is reportedly is a state of disbelief and says:

> "These people are supposed to be protecting us from
> terrorists. I'm just relieved these top-secret images didn't
> fall into the wrong hands."

Rosie (18, from Middlesex)

02 March 2009

Amy G is allegedly "alarmed" that "terrorists could be using Google Maps to snoop on our secret naval bases". This follows earlier concerns that Google Maps might be used by unspecified evil-doers to target army bases, and presumably the lost city of Atlantis (see Page 27).

> "Google Earth allows us to view the world from our homes.
> But access should be restricted if terrorists are using it."
>
> *Amy G (20, from Sheffield)*

21 August 2009

Today we are told that Danni is "shocked" at news that convicted Lockerbie bomber Abdelbaset al-Megrahi has been released from jail and allowed to return to Libya on 'compassionate grounds' after being diagnosed with terminal prostate cancer:

> "It's all very well showing mercy, but he was
> convicted of mass murder."
>
> *Danni (22, from Coventry)*

It later emerged that the release was linked to a proposed £400million arms deal with Libya, because mercy is for the weak and missile defence systems don't sell themselves.

Al-Megrahi died on 20 May 2012, almost three years after his release, and exactly six months after Libyan dictator Muammar Gaddafi was dragged from his hiding place in a roadside culvert and lynched by a mob.

'Our Boys'

12 January 2004

There's a lot of these, for likely reasons that we have already discussed at the top of this chapter, so we're just going to go open bolt, rapid-fire, until we empty the magazine and freedom reigns.

Today, Zoe is allegedly "upset to hear that Col Tim Collins is leaving the Army" and apparently says:

> "He is a born leader and I'm sure that whatever he
> does he will get some well-deserved respect."
>
> *Zoe (22, from London)*

08 April 2004

Zoe also reportedly thinks that it "defies belief" that "defence chiefs spent £259million on Chinook helicopters that cannot* fly when it is cloudy" and is on record as saying:

> "It's another example of bumbling bureaucrats failing Our Boys on the frontline. When will they learn?"
>
> *Zoe (22, from London)*

(*Cost-cutting and British defence safety standards collided here to result in the procurement of a vehicle that was technically capable of flying in the presence of clouds, but not permitted to without an expensive overhaul and/or the fully digital cockpit that many think should have been included in the original order.)

12 July 2004

Melanie is described as "fuming" at the idea that "defence chiefs have spent £3million on 3,000 fancy office chairs," presumably at the expense of "thousands of brave soldiers (who) have to buy their own boots and sleeping bags, and face shortages of equipment," and says:

> "This is a disgrace. Any spare cash should be going to soldiers."
>
> *Melanie (22, from Watford)*

27 August 2004

Zoe is reported to be in a state of disbelief about "petty" council bosses who allegedly "refused to fly a town hall flag at half mast in honour of a local soldier killed in Iraq" and admonishes:

> "I'm sure it would have given his family some comfort in their time of grief. It is so petty to refuse them that small gesture."
>
> *Zoe (22, from London)*

18 March 2005

Today, we are told that Nicola T is "awestruck by the bravery" of Private Johnson Beharry, who has recently been awarded the Victoria Cross:

> "To put your life at risk the way he did, not once but twice, deserves the very highest honour."
>
> *Nicola T (22, from London)*

12 December 2005

Katie is allegedly "impressed by the heroics" of Katrina Hodge, an 18-year-old military clerk who disarmed an Iraqi rebel:

> "What a gal! She's got a lot of guts for someone her age, Katrina's actions prove women can be just as good as men in the Army."

Katie (22, from Liverpool)

02 February 2006

Katie is also reportedly "chuffed" for "the two lesbians who have become the first serving soldiers to get hitched" and says:

> "Good for them. I hope they are really happy together."

Katie (21, from Liverpool)

You may also note that Katie had an un-birthday between this editorial and the last, going from age 22 to 21. This happened frequently on Page 3, with the models' ages being revised as casually as the use-by dates on expired meat in a dodgy convenience store.

17 April 2008

We are reliably informed that Keeley is "disgusted" at the sight of "the awful barracks for our brave soldiers in Brize Norton" and has this to say about it:

> "It's a disgrace. Our servicemen put their lives on the line for our country. They deserve to be treated better."

Keeley (21, from Bromley)

22 April 2008

Sam is reportedly "amazed" by the recovery of Afghanistan hero Ben McBean, who has been described by Prince Harry as a "real hero" after losing his left arm and right leg in a landmine blast:

> "He's a real inspiration and a hero - not just to Harry, but to all of us. The way he's back up and walking already is simply unbelievable. I'm so pleased he got to meet Harry again."

Sam (22, from Manchester)

03 June 2008

Vikki is reportedly "delighted" by "the Sun-backed Help for Heroes fund to build a therapy pool and gym for injured troops" hitting £6million:

> "Being able to give them the best facilities to recover is really important and will help these brave heroes massively."
>
> *Vikki (20, from Essex)*

05 June 2008

General Sir Richard Dannatt has called for a pay rise for soldiers after discovering that traffic wardens get paid more than those risking their lives on the frontline, and "pretty Peta" agrees:

> "It's not right that traffic wardens earn more than Our Boys. They do a fantastic job and fully deserve a decent rise."
>
> *Peta (21, from Essex)*

25 June 2008

Keeley is allegedly "stunned" that "the Yanks have dubbed our brave soldiers 'scruffy' and urged them to get haircuts":

> "Almost every soldier I've met has neat hair and cares about their appearance, so this criticism seems strange."
>
> *Keeley (22, from Bromley)*

I am not sure what happened with the haircuts, if anything, but I do know that there was a later dispute between top brass and frontline soldiers who complained that instructions for wearing the new MTP (Multi-Terrain Pattern) uniform "undermined morale, discipline and professionalism," and wanted a return to tucked-in shirts and neatly-rolled sleeves.

21 July 2008

"Dog-lover Rhian" is reported to be "impressed with the German Shepherds which are being trained by the SAS to serve Britain" and supposedly quips:

> "It's amazing that they could help us in Afghanistan or Iraq. They're real dogs of war."
>
> *Rhian (21, from Manchester)*

12 August 2008

Today we are told that Jenny "applauded Para Lee Clegg for returning to frontline action in Afghanistan for the first time since he was cleared of murdering two Irish teenagers," before saying:

"I'm thrilled for him."

Jenny (18, from The Wirral)

01 September 2008

Sam is reportedly "delighted that our Armed Forces are to be honoured with The Sun Military Awards" and says:

"We should all remember the sacrifices they
make for us every day."

Sam (22, from Manchester)

08 September 2008

Nikkala is apparently "overjoyed that the Help for Heroes campaign has broken through the £10million barrier" and enthuses accordingly:

"I can't believe so much has been raised! Our
brave troops deserve the best treatment when
they come home and this will be a great help."

Nikkala (24, from Middlesex)

10 November 2008

There is the usual tabloid fuss about wearing a poppy that one expects every year at this time, as things get ugly for any MP or TV presenter who has dared to forget to remember.

It is in this context that we are informed that Katie has "joined the millions across Britain who showed their support for the poppy appeal" by saying:

"It was great to see large turn-outs at services across
the land. It's vital we never forget those who gave
their lives for this country."

Katie (23, from Liverpool)

12 November 2008

Today we are reliably assured that "Sam felt proud to see three World War One survivors honouring fallen comrades 90 years after the conflict," before saying:

> "We owe so much to these brave men and all those who have made sacrifices for us. They must never be forgotten."
>
> *Sam (22, from Manchester)*

17 December 2008

Katie "salutes the winners of our first Sun Military Awards - The Millies" who were "honoured in London last night" in a soon-to-be-televised ceremony presented by Tess Daly:

> "This is just the sort of recognition our brave servicemen and women deserve for their heroism."
>
> *Katie Leigh (20, from Birmingham)*

24 December 2008

It is a bleak and challenging time for British military personnel in Afghanistan, and in response, members of the public have been sending unsolicited Christmas and care parcels addressed "to a soldier"... despite the Ministry of Defence asking them very nicely not to, because a 60% increase in mail delivery is overburdening their parcel system. So today Keeley hopes that "British troops on the frontline in Afghanistan... receive well-wishers' gifts in time for Christmas" and says:

> "We should do everything in our power to help them enjoy the festive period."
>
> *Keeley (22, from Bromley)*

17 March 2009

Last week, there was a small but angry group protesting at a soldiers' homecoming parade in Luton. It was an ugly and misjudged demonstration complete with upset, unrest and arrest, but today Rosie is reportedly "thrilled to see 20,000 people cheering a parade of soldiers in Leicester" and reports as if from the scene:

> "It was great to witness after the ugly scenes in Luton last week. Our troops need all the support they can get."
>
> *Rosie (18, from Middlesex)*

25 March 2009

Today Katie is "pleased to see our troops getting the chance to meet England footie stars" and says:

> "It was a nice gesture by the FA. England players are often seen as heroes, but they met REAL heroes yesterday."

Katie (23, from Liverpool)

26 March 2009

Nikkala is described as "proud of the Royal Marines' latest victory in Afghanistan" and reportedly has this to share:

> "Our Boys in 42 Commando have shown the Taliban what the bulldog spirit is all about. Well done lads. You're true heroes."

Nikkala (25, from Middlesex)

30 March 2009

We are assured that Danni "is fully behind The Sun's new Help for Heroes campaign to raise £20million" and issued the following statement accordingly:

> "Our injured troops deserve every penny to improve their treatment and standard of living. Together we can reach that target."

Danni (21, from Coventry)

23 July 2009

Conservative party leader and PM hopeful David Cameron has proposed a scheme offering free live entertainment and events to all serving military personnel, and veterans recently discharged through injury. Today, Keeley "salutes the plan to give Our Boys and Girls free tickets to top sports events and gigs" and says:

> "They risk their lives for our freedom, so it's right we should thank them in this special way. It's a great way for society to say thank you."

Keeley (22, from Bromley)

To Cameron's credit, the not-for-profit company 'Tickets for Troops' was up and running within a few months and remains active today.

05 August 2009

Amii is allegedly "fuming" over reports that "armoured vehicles which would save the lives of British soldiers are lying idle" and admonishes:

> "It's a disgrace that these trucks are left
> stranded while Our Boys are dodging bullets
> and bombs on the front line."

Amii (22, from Birmingham)

07 August 2009

Danni is reportedly "backing Marine Ben McBean's battle to receive compensation from the MoD for his war injuries" and has this to say:

> "MoD chiefs should be ashamed of themselves for
> not treating Ben like the true hero he is."

Danni (22, from Coventry)

10 August 2009

Today we are told that Katie is "appalled to hear that our soldiers in Afghanistan have been forced to dye their shorts for camouflage" and says:

> "They have been let down by the Ministry
> again. It's outrageous."

Katie (23, from Liverpool)

The NHS

The NHS is a tough nut to crack, but Tories and tabloids have found that with persistence comes results. On the PR front, all you have to do is starve the target of positive coverage and just wait for the relentless negative coverage to take its toll.

03 November 2003

Government-imposed time targets and a rise in emergency calls have combined to create queues of patient-filled ambulances clogging A&E entrances. At present, patients who are not ready to be admitted to A&E wait in an ambulance, and this has an obvious knock-on effect on crucial paramedic response times.

Two ambulance trusts have responded to the problem with a plan to use existing decontamination equipment to alleviate the bottleneck: large, heated inflatable tents are readily available and can be used as a temporary waiting station for patients, leaving ambulances free to respond to other calls.

Sadly, all some people see is the indignity of sitting in a tent, and not the plan's potential to solve the more crucial problem of response times... and it is on this note that we meet Michelle, who is reportedly "furious with the deal NHS patients get" and says:

> "We seem to rank as a Third World nation on healthcare.
> To think that patients have to be treated in tents and
> that a dying pensioner waits an hour for an ambulance is
> disgraceful - especially when you consider how much tax
> we pay into the NHS."
>
> *Michelle (20, from Oldham)*

22 March 2004

Who needs bingo when you've got Superbug league tables? Today, Melanie says this of "shock new MRSA figures" showing a 3.6% increase in blood infections:

> "People need to feel safe in hospital. There's a growing
> feeling hygiene standards on the wards are not as high
> as they were a generation ago. With all the money
> thrown at the NHS recently it's startling to see a killer
> bug spread so rapidly."
>
> *Melanie (22, from Watford)*

15 March 2005

If you thought tents were bad, brace yourselves. Today, Ruth is reportedly "horrified to learn patients are being housed in offices" and says:

> "It's quite disgraceful that this should happen because there is no room on the wards. How would NHS bosses like that to happen to their sick relatives?"
>
> *Ruth (22, from Kent)*

28 March 2005

Luke Day, the youngest victim of MRSA in Britain, died on 3 February 2005. He was just 36 hours old. Luke's parents have since accused Ipswich Hospital of a cover-up over poor standards of hygiene.

Nearly two months later, the source of this lone infection in the maternity unit remains a mystery, but The Sun have published photos of dust under a bed or something, which answers all of the questions.

And so we arrive here at the point where today's topless model Zoe is allegedly "horrified that the hospital where a newborn baby recently died of MRSA is still filthy" and has this to say:

> "Nothing appears to have been learned from Luke Day's death. Someone has to take responsibility and clean up our hospitals."
>
> *Zoe (24, from London)*

06 February 2006

A government campaign aimed at improving hygiene, detection and awareness has so far failed to cut MRSA infection rates, so today Freya is reportedly "horrified by the MRSA scandal" and apparently thinks that a multi-authority problem can be solved with a single sudsy solution:

> "The NHS spends a fortune on pen-pushing executives. They would be better off swapping their computers for a mop and bucket."
>
> *Freya (18, from Nottingham)*

I'm sure you'll all be delighted to know that 'pen pushing' eventually paid off, with MRSA infection rates being cut from 1.8% of patients in 2006 to less than 0.1% by 2011. The method of using healthcare executives as cleaners was never tested.

19 April 2006

Becky & Mel are as loved-up as ever, but today they are additionally "shocked to learn some GPs rake in £250,000 a year," prompting Becky to say:

> "They do a tough job and deserve to be rewarded,
> but the NHS should not be over-spending."
>
> *Becky (24, from London)*

06 June 2006

A government watchdog has revealed that a total of 2,159 people have died after "patient safety incidents" in the last year (April 2005 to March 2006) and that a further 4,529 patients suffered "severe harm" through avoidable mistakes. Even these numbers need to be balanced against the fact that the leading form of incident is "patient accident" (at 39.2%) but the wider numbers are also worth a closer look. Of a total of 526,599 patients reportedly experiencing a 'safety incident', 68.6% of them (361,464) suffered "no harm" and 24.7% (130,086) suffered "low harm". That's 93.3% at low-to-no harm after a safety incident, compared to 1.3% dead or seriously fucked up.

But today in The Sun, the focus is on the biggest number, which (a) has been worryingly conflated with the risk of death or severe harm, and (b) has further been inflated to "near to a million" through the novel method of casually straying outside the annual figures and rounding up like there's no tomorrow for most of us. It is in this context that Katie is reportedly in a state of disbelief "that nearly a million patients were killed or injured in hospital blunders last year" and says:

> "In this day and age people need to feel they are going to
> be looked after in hospitals, not putting themselves at risk."
>
> *Katie (21, from Liverpool)*

(Source for all figures: National Patient Safety Agency, Quarterly National Reporting and Learning System, Summer 2006)

20 May 2008

A small NHS trust tried to back up 10 years worth of data covering 38,000 patients, but the disc was mislaid by a courier company. Rhian is reported to be "alarmed" at the loss of the disc and wrongly claims it "vanished in the post" before saying:

> "The disc lists people's drinking habits and other
> highly personal conditions. It's an outrage - someone
> must be held accountable."
>
> *Rhian (20, from Manchester)*

15 October 2008

We are reliably informed that Vikki "can't believe the staggering £12billion claims bill the NHS is facing as a result of blunders" and says:

> "These mistakes should not happen, but the compensation culture is a huge drain on the health sector. At the end of the day taxpayers like me foot the bill."

> *Vikki (20, from Essex)*

30 January 2009

Today, Rosie reportedly "had a shiver when she heard about the hospital which has called in an exorcist" before saying:

> "It's the kind of thing you normally only hear about in films. But fair play to the hospital for taking staff concerns seriously."

> *Rosie (18, from Middlesex)*

Politicians

In this chapter, you should worry less about the prejudices for and against individual politicians (that are probably just filtering into the Page 3 changing rooms through some innocent and entirely organic form of social osmosis), and more about the extent to which your typical topless model obsesses over current events and the minutiae of party/political campaign strategies. Allegedly.

Iain Duncan Smith

06 October 2003

Today we are informed that the 'stunning' Michelle "reckons Iain Duncan Smith has to get tough at the Tory conference this week" and says:

> "One thing IDS has got to do is get stuck in like a real politician and carry the fight to Labour. He's been a bit weedy in the past and needs to go on the attack. I'd like to hear how he is going to tackle important issues like pensions, transport and education. We're all fed up of talk and want some action."

Michelle (20, from Oldham)

IDS briefly impressed The Sun with some anti-EU rhetoric (see Page 45), but within a few days it was all over bar the shouting for the self-described "quiet man".

10 October 2003

The Tory conference is over. We are informed that Nicola T "was among viewers who thought little of Iain Duncan Smith's address to the Tory faithful," and further advised that she has this to say:

> "It was like a school play. The whole thing was just so stage-managed. I half-expected to catch sight of someone holding boards up for the audience saying 'clap' and 'cheer'. As a voter I was left feeling totally disinterested. He's boring and as soon as the Tories get rid of him, the better it will be for them."

Nicola T (21, from London)

The Tories got rid of IDS less than two weeks later. Michael Howard was next in line.

Michael Howard

31 October 2003

Today we are assured that Nicola T thinks "Michael Howard will be a success as Tory leader" and says:

> "IDS was bald and bland and never going to be a figurehead for the Tories. Now you've got a man who is married to a gorgeous ex-model and looks the part."
>
> *Nicola T (21, from London)*

26 January 2005

Demonstrating that it's not only about charisma and 'hot-wife' status, today Jak "thinks there's nothing racist about protecting Britain's borders" and says:

> "We're a small island nation and we're already over-crowded. Michael Howard's view on immigration is shared throughout the country. It simply makes sense."
>
> *Jak (19, from Tunbridge Wells)*

Nick Griffin

10 June 2008

Of course, there's such a thing as taking it too far, so today Keeley "reckons BNP leader Nick Griffin got what he deserved when he was pelted with eggs" and says:

> "The BNP may have had election success, but their views don't have any place in politics."
>
> *Keeley (22, from Bromley)*

21 May 2009

Further, Peta is "outraged" at the idea that BNP leader Nick Griffin might be included with other MEPs as a guest at a Buckingham Palace garden party and says:

> "I find BNP policies deeply offensive. He should have no place at an event such as this."
>
> *Peta (22, from Essex)*

Tony Blair

04 May 2005

Ruth reportedly "thinks it's heart-warming that Tony and Cherie Blair have such a strong, loving marriage" and says:

> "It can only be good for Britain - a stable Prime Minister means a stable country."

Ruth (22, from Kent)

This is a notably restrained mini-editorial given that the front page story it supports compares the size of Blair's massive majority to his penis and features an interview where he jokingly brags about giving it to Cherie five times a night (yes, really), but at least she's got her tits out for the occasion.

27 September 2006

Zoe allegedly hails Tony Blair's Labour Party conference speech as "simply the best" and says:

> "What a performance! He showed all the qualities that attracted millions of voters in 1997. It will be very interesting to see whether his departure rebounds on Labour come the next election."

Zoe (24, from London)

13 November 2006

Today 'sexy' Ami is described as "sad to see the Prime Minister booed at yesterday's TUC conference" and is further alleged to have said:

> "Delegates were daft to jeer and walk out when Blair was speaking. I'm just glad Gordon Brown backed Blair on this occasion."

Ami (19, from Birmingham)

Sadly for the Page 3 ladies, Tony Blair has by this time acknowledged the many calls for him to step down and has even spoken the words "my last Conference as Leader," so it's only a matter of time before he announces his leaving date, and by now all sorts of people are starting to lose patience with him... but it will take The Sun and Page 3 another five months before they finally decide to cough politely in his direction.

02 May 2007

After much waiting, today we are told that Ami "can't wait for Tony Blair to announce his leaving date," and says as nicely as possible:

> "It's the end of an era and exciting times are ahead.
> The whole country is waiting for the next chapter - so
> the sooner Blair lets us in on his plans the better."
>
> *Ami (20, from Birmingham)*

11 May 2007

However, none of this stops Danni from allegedly paying tribute to Tony Blair's ten years of service as Prime Minister before saying:

> "The country has benefited tremendously from his
> leadership, courage and drive."
>
> *Danni (19, from Coventry)*

Tony Blair finally resigned as Prime Minister on 27 June, and was succeeded by Gordon Brown, who the Page 3 models did not fancy anywhere near as much.

David Blunkett

It was not widely known or documented at the time, but Rebekah Wade/Brooks and David Blunkett were very close friends, as well as political allies. We're talking proper chums here, folks.

Here I will remind you that - ethically speaking - the ideal form of an editorial on Page 3 is where the model appearing in that day's issue is permitted to nominate the topic of her choice *and* express her own opinion on that topic. If any editor or sub-editor were to dictate or direct otherwise, it would (a) destroy any claim that Page 3 was an empowering platform, and (b) undermine the editorial content of the entire newspaper, as one could never be sure that the same wasn't happening to Jeremy Clarkson or anyone else on their platform with a great big pair of tits.

It certainly would not do for the main editor to dictate the topic and content of a series of editorials in order to protect a friend who is about to be revealed as a key player in the kind of sex scandal that The Sun normally throws itself into with barely restrained glee. That would reveal the entire venture as a sham.

All of that said, we cannot discount the possibility that any or all of the following is down to coincidence and/or the remarkably likeability of a former Home Secretary and the everyman appeal of his forward-thinking policies.

13 August 2004

Two days from now, the News of the World will host a soft-pedalling exclusive revealing that David Blunkett has been engaged in a "passionate" three-year affair with a married woman. However, none of this is in the public domain yet; we only have the possibility that editor Rebekah Wade/Brooks may have heard what her sister title was up to, and/or may have been told something about it by her best friend. So, there's no reason for Page 3 to say anything about Blunkett just yet, but it is odd that today's editorial praises a recent Home Office initiative, as we are told that Leah "reckons it's a good idea to make every offence arrestable" and says:

> "There's no point just ticking people off. This proposal
> will make a lot more people stay within the law."
>
> *Leah (22, from Hastings)*

On Sunday (15 August) NOTW went live with their exclusive, casting it as the story of a hard-working Home Secretary led astray by his well-meaning heart. The Sun followed this up with a series of items designed to cast former lover Kimberley Quinn as a heartless, scheming monster out to wreck Blunkett's career. Each of these angles promoted the premise that the good work Mr Blunkett was doing in the Home Office was far more important than any questions one might have about what he was doing with his penis. Both narratives were so rich, they often crowded out any mention of Quinn's husband and what he might think of it all.

16 August 2004

It's Monday. Everybody else is talking about what Mr Blunkett has been doing with his penis, but today on Page 3 the topless model wants readers to know that the Home Office should get to work and "get tough of benefit cheats":

> "I am staggered how they are ripping off the country.
> The Government should come down very hard on
> anyone making fraudulent claims."
>
> *Melanie (22, from Watford)*

17 August 2004

Tuesday. Still nothing about David Blunkett, but here's another Home Office initiative, as Nikkala "supports the government initiative to try and save criminals' children from lives of crime" and says:

> "Anything that helps them avoid making the same
> mistakes as their parents has to be a good thing."
>
> *Nikkala (22, from Middlesex)*

16 December 2004

And that's pretty much our lot until we arrive at this point - four months later - not to bury Caesar, but to praise him. Today, we are told that Katie "was devastated to hear David Blunkett had quit" and has this to say about his departure:

> "I think it's terrible that a man who has done so much for his country has felt it necessary to leave public office. Blunkett was one of the few Home Secretaries prepared to get tough on issues that matter to ordinary people - asylum, terrorism and law and order."

Katie (19, from Liverpool)

David Blunkett moved on to work in entirely the same field within exactly the same party and under the very same leader when he returned as Secretary of State for Work and Pensions immediately after the 2005 election... but by then, he had already secured the shares and directorship that would ultimately lead to his second downfall.

03 November 2005

Danni is described as "sorry to see David Blunkett resign" and has this to say:

> "There was no denying David's abilities as a Cabinet minister. It was a typical gesture of him to resign for the sake of his Cabinet colleagues. But in doing so the Government is a far poorer place."

Danni (18, from Coventry)

On 30 November 2005, The Sun announced that David Blunkett's "forthright and outspoken views on life and politics" would be aired in a weekly column every Thursday. Blunkett would later sign a further contract with News International as an adviser on 'corporate social responsibility'. Meanwhile, The Sun thought little of Blunkett's successors in his beloved Home Office, and Page 3 wasn't shy about it:

25 January 2007

Today, Nikkala is reportedly "astounded that the Home Office is in such a terrible state" and says:

> "John Reid is a joke. We have dangerous criminals on the run, foreign prisoners let out - now jails are full. What next?"

Nikkala (24, from Middlesex)

John Prescott

27 April 2006

Today, we are told that Becky thinks "Romeo Prescott's not her type of bloke" and says this about his sex appeal:

> "I imagine he thinks a good date is a few pints
> of bitter and a steak pie at his local - I prefer
> my men a bit smoother."

Becky (24, from London)

As you can see, for reasons that are not entirely clear, Page 3 take a rather different position and tone when John Prescott is caught doing things with his penis that do not involve his wife. This editorial is from the day before Prescott admitted the affair, and already there is relevant commentary from a topless model that draws our eyes away from his work in government and even the detail of the allegations to focus instead on what an unattractive mate he is.

07 July 2006

Further, rather than staying out of the whole affair like many other Page 3 models in the very recent past, today 'gorgeous' Zoe allegedly steps forward to bluntly announce "John Prescott should quit" and says:

> "There are big questions over the casino row and Prezza
> hasn't denied rumours of other affairs. He's in big trouble
> and is doing a lot of damage to the PM and Government."

Zoe (24, from London)

Needless to say, there was no Page 3 editorial lamenting Precott's departure.

Gordon Brown

23 March 2006

Keeley reportedly believes that today's budget "shows how desperate Gordon Brown is to be in No. 10" and says:

> "He's giving away money so voters will back him.
> But is it a budget on the never-never from a
> Chancellor who might never be PM?"

Keeley (18, from Bromley)

10 May 2006

Like many people, Gordon Brown is becoming impatient with Blair over his refusal to name a departure date, and in recent interviews, he has issued carefully worded warnings about potentially unstable, disorderly and/or undignified transitions.

There has been much gnashing of teeth in response, but what is eventually extracted is a semi-public assurance through underlings of a provisional date of summer 2007 (or early 2008 at the latest).

So today Becky and Mel appear as a happy couple to announce that they are "pleased to learn of Tony Blair and Gordon Brown's peace pact," but Becky warns:

> "Gordon's behaved like a spoiled child. I hope he
> doesn't when he's at No. 10."

Becky (24, from London)

14 September 2006

Last week, Tony Blair announced that he would step down as PM within a year. He declined to give a precise date, but Brown finally has what he wants: a finite commitment and a deadline that cannot be passed without Blair being called to account. Blair's still being difficult about a precise departure date, but all of the fuss has gone out of the fight.

It is in this context that we learn that Zoe is "relieved that Tony Blair and Gordon Brown have finally ended their rift" and says:

> "Hopefully they can get on with running the country
> and end all the bad blood. I think the whole bust-up
> didn't do them - or Labour - any favours."

Zoe (24, from London)

01 May 2007

Sam is reported to be "pleased to hear Gordon Brown praising Tony Blair so highly yesterday" and says:

> "It's taken long enough, but in Mr Blair's final
> months it's good to see a united front."

Sam (21, from Manchester)

By now you may have noticed that early Page 3 editorials about Gordon Brown were mostly about Tony Blair. This would not change until Blair left... when suddenly this same series of topless models became obsessed with the subject of Brown's ailing premiership.

27 November 2007

Today we are informed that Zoe "wasn't surprised to learn that Labour general secretary Peter Watt had resigned over the secret donations scandal" and we are further advised that she "reckons PM Gordon Brown can expect another battering" as a result:

> "Things really are going from bad to worse for the
> Prime Minister. He's gone from being untouchable to
> looking like a man who is in deep trouble."

Zoe (25, from London)

04 August 2008

Sam is reportedly "amused by the PM's fitness drive" and says:

> "It sounds like he's taking the idea of a leadership
> fight literally. But a six-pack won't stop inflationary
> pressures or a property downturn."

Sam (22, from Manchester)

15 September 2008

Today, Peta is described as "amazed that a dozen MPs want a leadership challenge to oust troubled PM Gordon Brown" and says:

> "Without him running the country, who could Labour
> turn to as the person to win over voters."

Peta (21, from Essex)

You may be wondering why the sudden change in tone. Look at the date: a global financial crisis is in progress. This doesn't yet doesn't stop The Sun from calling Brown 'troubled', but in a little over a week (and for roughly two weeks after that), blame would briefly switch to the 'troubled times'.

24 September 2008

Sam is reportedly "impressed by Gordon Brown's conference speech" and says:

> "It was clever, full of coded messages to his opponents.
> Mr Brown came out fighting and Labour may stand by
> him for now in these troubled economic times."

Sam (22, from Manchester)

11 January 2009

The immediate crisis has more or less passed and is about to quietly segue into a global recession that everybody can enjoy.

Meanwhile, Page 3 is right back to where they were for most of their yesterdays, which is bashing Brown like there's no tomorrow. Today, Sam is reported to be "among the voters who feel let down by Labour" and says:

> "They've had their chance and not taken it.
> They've wasted a lot of time in government, so it's
> time for someone else to have a go at solving
> Britain's problems."

> *Sam (23, from Manchester)*

06 May 2009

Today we are assured that Vikki "isn't surprised that Gordon Brown may reshuffle his cabinet" and has this to say:

> "The Prime Minister must do something quickly or
> he'll lose the election. Perhaps a change of personnel
> at the top could change his party's fortunes around."

> *Vikki (20, from Essex)*

15 May 2009

Poppy is reportedly "not surprised that support for Labour is at an all-time low" and we are told that she has this to say about it::

> "The Government has been losing public
> confidence for months - and to cap it all we've had
> the scandal of MP's expenses."

> *Poppy (18, from Somerset)*

18 May 2009

Today we are reliably informed that Becky "wants Gordon Brown to call an election" and says:

> "Why doesn't the Prime Minister let us decide if
> his Government is still fit for purpose?"

> *Becky (25, from London)*

03 June 2009

Today Rosie apparently expresses concern about "the exodus of top Labour politicians" because it "piles more pressure on Gordon Brown to stand down":

"Losing the Home Secretary and several others adds
to the sense of panic engulfing his government."

Rosie (18, from Middlesex)

04 June 2009

Peta is allegedly "amazed that Gordon Brown could be ditched as Prime Minister by email" and says:

"The Labour rebels who want Gordon to resign
should be brave enough to identify themselves
instead of signing anonymous emails."

Peta (22, from Essex)

09 June 2009

Danni reportedly thinks Gordon Brown "has given himself breathing space after his speech to MPs last night" but warns:

"He's still got a lot to do if he's going to survive - and
if Labour is to avoid a General Election hammering."

Danni (22, from Coventry)

Brown did avoid an outright hammering, but not an ultimate loss to a coalition government headed by David Cameron.

David Cameron

05 October 2006

Today we are told that Danni "reckons David Cameron's first keynote speech as Tory leader showed promise" but we are further assured that she adds:

"I think the public need to hear him focus more
on policies and less on presentation if the
Tories are going to realistically challenge
Labour at the next election."

Danni (19, from Coventry)

30 January 2008

At this point in so-called history, Cameron mostly earns mentions in The Sun through pledges and speeches about getting tough on this or that, and today on Page 3 is no different, as Keeley is allegedly "delighted that Tory leader David Cameron has pledged to tackle street crime," and says:

> "It's about time a politician took a tougher stance
> over the rise of violence. Nowadays streets are so
> mean that you don't feel safe walking down them.
> David is right to get tough."

> *Keeley (21, from Kent)*

25 July 2008

But it's not all violent crime and immigrants and illegal asylum seekers. Good old-fashioned home-grown theft can strike anybody at any time, and today we are informed that Rosie is "impressed that Tory leader David Cameron went online to report his bike stolen" and further has this to say about it:

> "He could have used his position to make a fuss,
> but instead he did the right thing."

> *Rosie (17, from Sunbury)*

See? He's not all that posh and elitist and out of touch. Maybe.

What Page 3 failed to mention at the time was that Cameron chained his bike to a 3-foot-high free-standing bollard, neglecting to predict that a thief might simply lift his bike over the top, chain and all, before making off with it. Which they did.

Cameron would later go on to deploy the same care, wit and caution when 'safely' delivering the EU referendum his backbenchers had been demanding of him since he took over as party leader.

02 October 2008

Peta reportedly thinks that David Cameron's Conservative Party conference speech "was very inspiring" and says:

> "We are all a bit down in the dumps, feeling the credit
> card pinch. He spoke with passion and from the heart
> and maybe he is just what the country needs."

> *Peta (21, from Essex)*

The Sun would later formally switch its allegiance to the Conservatives, but not until the end of September 2009, a month after Wade/Brooks retired as editor.

Jacques Chirac

25 November 2003

It is the week after Bush's state visit to the UK. In the face of massive protests over his foreign policy and the ongoing disaster in Iraq, Bush had to conduct the entire visit behind locked gates and closed doors.

However, this week, Tony Blair plays host to French President Jacques Chirac, who gets to inspect a guard of honour by the first Battalion of the Grenadier Guards - with no-one yelling at him - and The Sun is pissed.

It is in this context that we are assured that today's topless model Anna was so "appalled" at the sight of the inspection ceremony that she said:

> "It was about time he was introduced to
> Our Boys - real soldiers. He shied away from
> Iraq. Maybe he took notes yesterday to pass
> on to French troops."
>
> *Anna (22, from London)*

George W. Bush

There was, fittingly enough, scant mention of Bush on Page 3. This may have had something to do with sensitivities evident when Bush visited this country (Page 3 was suspended for that day) or it may have been the result of random chance. We may never know.

However, there are many editorials that voice full support for his initiatives in the Middle East and his arguments in support of military action there, so he shouldn't feel too bad about the overall lack of name-checks on Page 3 if it's causing him any concern in his retirement.

Barack Obama

06 November 2008

Today Page 3 informs us that Keeley "has been visiting Hollywood," and while there was "bowled over by the massive wave of support for Barack Obama". She reports:

> "He'll be a fantastic president. Obama is
> such an inspirational figure to so many
> people across the globe."
>
> *Keeley (22, from Bromley)*

19 January 2009

Danni is reportedly "amazed by the array of A-list stars who came out to back Barack Obama ahead of his inauguration" and says:

> "He has a huge task ahead of him. But he has
> the support of some top names."
>
> *Danni (21, from Coventry)*

21 January 2009

Today we are told that Keeley "could hardly contain her excitement yesterday as she watched Barack Obama being sworn in as the 44th US President".

Pictured in a stars-and-stripes bikini, she adds:

> "It's the biggest job in the world and Barack is the
> best man for that job. There are huge challenges
> ahead, but Obama is the right man at the right
> time. He's the kind of inspirational leader who can
> get the US back on track. Yes he can!"
>
> *Keeley (22, from Bromley)*

01 April 2009

Amy G is described as "thrilled" about Barack Obama's visit to the UK, and is particularly happy about the full Englishness of his breakfast:

> "When he was elected he brought hope. We need a bit
> of that to guide us through the G20 agenda. And a good
> old fry-up will stand him in good stead for a busy week."
>
> *Amy G (20, from Sheffield)*

Sarah Palin

04 September 2008

Today we're informed that Rhian is "full of praise for UC vice-presidential candidate Sarah Palin" as she prepares to address the Republican convention, and says:

> "She's an inspiration to women."
>
> *Rhian (21, from Manchester)*

The Royal Family

Murdoch's relationship with the British royal family is... complicated. On one hand, he shifts countless units by treating their personal lives as an all-access reality show, but on the other, he has a heartfelt commitment to meritocracy that's so strong, it almost extends kind of near to the very top of the global corporate and media empire he plans to leave to his children. Oh, and you may notice that his Page 3 ladies have been keeping a special eye on a certain red-haired prince...

12 November 2004

Today we are told that Melanie "can't resist all-action hunks," so is obviously "thrilled to see Prince William training with the crack fighters of the SAS," and says:

> "Wills is one of the most handsome fellas
> around, but seeing him with the SAS makes
> him even more fanciable."

Melanie (24, from Watford)

13 January 2005

Prince Harry has attended a costume party dressed as a Nazi. The news is so shocking that The Sun literally run out of room and have no space to report that after two long years, the search for WMDs in Iraq is formally at an end. On Page 3, Katie is "alarmed to see Prince Harry sporting a Nazi armband" and warns:

> "British people will be horrified by a Royal wearing
> such gear. The snap will send shockwaves around
> Britain. He really ought to know better."

Katie (19, from Liverpool)

11 February 2005

We are reliably informed that Danni "has been closely following news of Charles and Camilla's wedding" and has this to say about their upcoming nuptials:

> "They really seem to be in love and it's great that they've
> made this decision. Camilla is certainly not a princess like
> Diana but I'm sure everyone will warm to her."

Danni (18, from Coventry)

23 February 2005

And now we cross live to our newly inducted royal correspondent on Page 3, where Katie "thinks it's terrible the Queen won't be attending Prince Charles' wedding," and further postulates that this "must be a deliberate snub" before saying:

> "It must be awful to have your mother miss one of
> the biggest days of your life. And what a slap in
> the face to Camilla. I know a civil wedding is
> probably not what the Queen had in mind, but if
> it's good enough for the rest of us, why isn't it
> good enough for her?"
>
> *Katie (19, from Liverpool)*

10 March 2005

Today, Peta is reportedly "stunned to hear that Princess Michael gets a 17-room apartment in Kensington Palace for £69 a week" and says:

> "This will outrage the public. She should ne
> nicknamed Princess Cushy now."
>
> *Peta (18, from Essex)*

08 April 2005

Sarah airs her baps as she welcomes "Charles and Camilla's plan to confess their 'sins and wickedness' in a prayer tomorrow" and gushes:

> "Charlie's really brave. He must love Camilla if he's
> prepared to do that in front of millions watching
> on TV. I think once it's over, they should be left
> alone to enjoy a happy marriage."
>
> *Sarah (21, from Crawley)*

11 April 2005

It is the day after a royal wedding, but an air of disappointment dominates Page 3 as Zoe "reckons Prince Charles should have kissed Camilla in public" and says:

> "It's a shame he didn't give her a peck. It would
> have been a lovely show of affection."
>
> *Zoe (24, from London)*

15 April 2005

It is the week after a royal wedding, and we're still waiting for a kiss, but at least a ribbon has been cut or something. Keeley reportedly thinks "Camilla looked radiant yesterday on her first public engagement since marrying Charles" and says:

> "It must have been scary for her, but the
> public will grow to love Camilla."

Keeley (18, from Bromley)

17 June 2005

Katie is described as "impressed" that the Queen has bought an iPod, and says:

> "People always say the Royals are old fashioned,
> but this shows she is in touch with the times. But
> I'd be really intrigued to know what she has on her
> playlist. Maybe a few tracks by Queen."

Katie (20, from Liverpool)

Oh. My. Aching. Sides.

15 September 2005

In a wide-ranging interview to mark his 21st birthday, Prince Harry has expressed regret for the Nazi costume incident from his young and reckless years almost a year ago, and puts it down to "immaturity" that he hopes he has overcome by "growing up" since. On Page 3, Ruth is "very impressed by Prince Harry's frank interview" and has this to say:

> "He has clearly come a long way since his Nazi
> gaffe and seemed genuine in his apology. He has
> grown into a mature and honest young man."

Ruth (22, from Kent)

21 April 2006

'Gorgeous' Keeley reportedly "thinks the Queen is fantastic for 80" and says:

> "She does a wonderful job and looks amazing for
> her age. It's incredible that the pressures of
> monarchy haven't taken more of a toll."

Keeley (19, from Bromley)

26 December 2006

The Queen's annual Christmas message is now available for download as audio, Rhian is reportedly "among the million people who downloaded the Queen's speech," and she has this to say:

> "The Queen is an inspiration - particularly for her age.
> It's great that her speech was released as a podcast -
> it shows she is happy to move with the times."

> *Rhian (19, from Manchester)*

27 December 2006

Today we are informed of Ami's great admiration for Prince Harry, who is "incredibly brave" in her view for "wanting to serve in Iraq with his comrades," but...

> "I feel for Chelsy - it will be very tough on both of
> them if he's away for months on end. She'll worry
> about him constantly."

> *Ami (19, from Birmingham)*

15 January 2008

Peta* is described as "sad to learn from the Diana inquest that she had such a troubled life" and is further quoted as saying:

> "Di brought joy to so many, but couldn't
> find happiness herself."

> *Peta (20, from Essex)*

(*Presumably, Alanis Morissette was unavailable for comment.)

03 March 2008

Katie Marie is all smiles and tits out for the latest prince-in-the-military and his touchingly humble dismissal of individual praise:

> "Prince Harry may not think of himself as a hero
> after his tour of Afghanistan, but I think he is -
> along with every single member of our armed
> forces serving Britain around the world."

> *Katie Marie (19, from Middlesex)*

06 March 2008

Nikkala is reported to be "delighted to see Prince Harry out enjoying himself with Chelsy" and says:

> "He did an incredible job in Afghanistan and deserves to let his hair down. Harry and Chelsy look really happy to be back together - they must have missed each other terribly."
>
> *Nikkala (25, from Middlesex)*

14 October 2008

Keeley apparently "can't believe that Kate Middleton has been so daft to use her mobile phone while driving" and admonishes:

> "It doesn't set a good example. Surely Kate can afford a hands-free kit… or she could get Wills to buy her one."
>
> *Keeley (22, from Bromley)*

It wasn't too long ago that News of the World's royal editor Clive Goodman and private investigator Glenn Mulcaire were done for intercepting phone messages, so I'm surprised she's daft enough to use a mobile phone at all at this stage, but moving on...

27 October 2008

Today we're told Ruth "wishes Prince Harry the very best of British in his dream of flying helicopter gunships" and has the following message for his royal braveness:

> "Good on you, royal Highness. You've proved yourself once on the front line and now you're going back for more."
>
> *Ruth (24, from Kent)*

04 November 2008

Amy D allegedly "applauds Prince Charles' ambitious plan to save the world's rainforests" and says:

> "I'm impressed that someone with his wealth and privilege should still care so passionately about this kind of thing."
>
> *Amy D (20, from The Wirral)*

23 December 2008

Katie is reported to be "tickled to learn Prince Harry faces a year without booze as he trains to be a pilot" and says:

> "Poor Harry, we know he likes a drink. But I've no doubt he will do it - he's a dedicated soldier."

Katie (23, from Liverpool)

12 January 2009

Video footage has been obtained by News of the World showing Prince Harry, when still an officer cadet at Sandhurst military academy, referring to one cadet as a "raghead" and another as "our little Paki friend."

St James's Palace has since issued an apology from the young prince, noting that he spoke "about a friend and without malice."

Today, Keeley apparently thinks "Prince Harry did the right thing by making a swift apology for using a racist word" and is certain that we can all move on:

> "He made a mistake, but hopefully he'll learn from it and that's the end of it."

Keeley (22, from Bromley)

26 January 2009

Nikkala is reportedly "not surprised that Prince Harry and Chelsy have split" and we are further informed that she has this to share:

> "It's a shame, but they are living very different lives. Mind you, plenty of girls will be delighted that Harry is a free agent again!"

Nikkala (23, from Middlesex)

13 July 2009

Keeley is said to be "amazed to hear that Prince Harry and his pilot pals blew £400 on booze in an hour" but allegedly offers the following for your consideration:

> "Everyone is allowed to let their hair down now and again - and this kind of thing will also help morale."

Keeley (22, from Bromley)

UFOs

It's not a crime to look up and wonder if we're not alone, and nor should it be.

20 June 2008

Ruth reportedly thinks "it was amazing that a police helicopter crew reported a UFO" and says:

> "People have been saying for years that they exist.
> You've got to admit, that if the police say so too,
> that's pretty convincing evidence."

Ruth (25, from Kent)

If you'll pardon my cynicism here, having 'evidence of an unidentified flying object' is like having rock solid proof of something or other.

Anyway, getting back to watching the skies...

25 June 2008

Today, Amii is described as "spooked by reports that UFOs were spotted over Shropshire" and we are told that she has this to say in response:

> "I've always been sceptical but these lights do
> look other-worldly. This could be real proof
> that we are not alone."

Amii (22, from Birmingham)

08 January 2009

Becky apparently "wasn't at all surprised to hear that a UFO may be responsible for damaging a wind turbine" and concludes:

> "A lot of people believe in UFOs - even Robbie
> Williams. Can they all be wrong?"

Becky (25, from London)

An object that may have been responsible for damage to a wind turbine remains unidentified, and it was able to interfere with that turbine because it was flying at the time. Oh, and Robbie Williams says aliens probably exist, so there's your answer.

15 January 2009

It's not all flying objects and flashing lights in the night sky, folks; we're talking real science here, from real scientists.

Today, Peta is reported to be "excited to hear that Nasa has new evidence of life on Mars" and says:

> "I always wondered if there was something out there and the discovery of methane on the planet is a significant find."
>
> *Peta (21, from Essex)*

03 February 2009

And finally, for all you doubters in the back row, here is Sam, allegedly "fascinated that humans could be descended from aliens," and reportedly in possession of a scientific theory:

> "Evidence for the theory of panspermia is compelling. It seems highly feasible our forerunners were cosmic microbes. That must be why we all need our own space."
>
> *Sam (23, from Manchester)*

War on Christmas

It's not a crime to believe in Santa, his elves or even all-powerful sky pixies, and nor should it be.

09 December 2004

The Sun is engaging in its annual practice of taking a season of goodwill and bleeding it for as much negative energy as possible. Today's front page story is the bold claim that nativity scenes and similar expressions of religious belief are being increasingly suppressed by "meddling politically correct jobsworths" determined to take the Christ out of Christmas by putting the Winter into Winterval, or something like that.

On Page 3, Krystle "reckons political correctness ruins the Christmas spirit" and projects her ample bosom into frame and then some:

> "Loony lefties who try to spoil Christmas
> should be banned. They all just seem to enjoy
> making other people miserable."
>
> *Krystle (21, from Manchester)*

There's no evidence to support the allegation of any conspiracy by the dreaded left to diminish Christmas in any way for anyone, and there never is, but that never stops these tabloid 'Christians' from pretending otherwise, because the one thing that being actively prejudiced teaches you is the strategic value of victim status.

Happily for The Sun, the very next day there is a fuss about a 'Posh & Becks' celebrity nativity scene stunt at Madame Tussauds. Without pausing for breath, The Sun shamelessly conflates the two issues, citing the 'Posh & Becks' fuss as evidence in support of their case. Quote The Sun: "It is supposed to be fun. But for some people, fun is a dirty word."

This tactic is undermined only by the inconvenient fact that all of the upset is over the inappropriateness of the appropriation of the religious symbolism... in a nativity scene that literally takes the alleged Christ out of his own Christmas.

Still, it's easy to become confused when the red mist rises and you can't think straight for the cacophony of the vast leftist media machine that's hell-bent against you and your little religious holiday, and The Sun are so serious about this that they essentially chide Tony Blair for denying his god by not coming to their aid and instead enlist the help of Michael Howard in their "campaign to save Christmas - by turning back the tide of politically correct meddling that threatens to destroy it."

The good Christian folk at The Sun continue their 'Save Our Christmas' campaign on Saturday with a FREE (if haughtily branded) nativity poster and news of an attack on the age-old tradition of celebrating Christmas with electric light, just like they did way back in Bible times.

Allow me to set the scene:

Hard-working citizen Vic Moszczynski's 8-foot-high Father Christmas sits among thousands of decorations illuminated by hundreds of lights. Mega-Santa switches between 'Jingle Bells' and 'We Wish You A Merry Christmas' while ten snowmen sing 'Santa Claus Is Coming To Town'. Sadly, an environmental health officer and a policeman have arrived to silence these electronic voices of faith and hope.

The Knapps of Gotherington, Gloucs. fare little better with their simple string of lights when an anonymous neighbour (obviously a leftist) drops a letter through their door that says: "Your dull, ugly front garden fails to reflect our village image."

So that's some people angry about too many decorations, and some people angry about not enough decorations. But it's still all about the self-described son of the alleged god of Abraham for some reason, because tabloids are never wrong, especially when it comes to honest hard-working god-fearing white people being victimised by the hated left.

15 December 2004

Today there's news of a further Christmas light display 'under attack' and the wider campaign continues as The Sun take the blessed nativity scene on the road, literally, on the back of a flatbed truck that they "defiantly" drive around London (totally not kidding) because the two assaults on our freedom are related somehow.

It is in this spirit that we hear 'gorgeous' Ruthie is "outraged to hear a Christmas fan had been sent hate mail for putting up decorations" and says:

> "It should be every person's right to celebrate
> whatever religious festival they want, however they
> want - so long as it does not infringe on others."

Ruthie (23, from Kent)

I do agree on this point. I also think that a woman who is alleged to have an empowering platform on the third page of a national newspaper should be able to use that platform as she sees fit.

So long as it does not infringe on others, obviously.

Page 3 on Page 3

Labour MP Clare Short was a long-standing critic of Page 3, arguing that it was exploitative pornography that did not belong in the mainstream. As far back as 1986 Short tried (unsuccessfully) to introduce a Commons bill outlawing the use of topless models in newspapers, and faced a campaign of harassment from both The Sun and News of the World as a result.

Then, in Short's own words, "nearly 20 years later, after I had left government, I was asked by a female journalist whether I still objected to Page 3, and I said I did (and) the bullying and intimidation started again."

The Sun's 2004 campaign against Clare Short was notably vicious, and of such a high priority to their editor(s) that it involved multiple front pages and a hotline 'poll' of their readers on par with campaigns against the EU and Abu Hamza.

Eight years later, Rebekah Wade/Brooks' successor Dominic Mohan appeared before the 2012 Leveson Inquiry to answer questions about this campaign and components of it that were needlessly personal and intimidating.

Facing questioning from Robert Jay Q.C. (Counsel to Inquiry), Mohan described The Sun's Page 3 models as "ambassadors for the paper" and "good role models," implying their widespread involvement in a range of "women's issues"... before deftly seeking to distance both himself and Wade/Brooks from the worst elements of an abusive and intrusive campaign targeting a female MP by saying she was fat and ugly and therefore motivated mainly if not wholly by jealously (though they probably meant 'envy', bless).

A sticking point in this exchange was abusive text in an editorial published under editor Wade/Brooks. Mohan responded to this with a further attempt at distance by saying: "... clearly 'fat and jealous' is in quotes. It is a quotation from somebody."

What the Leveson Inquiry did not hear from Mohan was that the people being quoted in the relevant editorial were all Page 3 models.

14 January 2004

Today Michelle is reportedly "furious over MP Clare Short's new rant about banning page 3" and says:

> "She should listen to my fans who tell me
> how much I brighten their day. She's just a
> jealous old battleaxe."
>
> *Michelle (20, from Oldham)*

Elsewhere in that same edition, more Page 3 girls are interviewed and their opinions are presented as follows:

"I think what she said is pathetic. Just because she's fat and ugly, doesn't mean to say we all have to cover up."

Nicola (21, from London)

"Page Three is fun, not porn. Everybody I know likes it, blokes and women alike."

Corina (19, from Oxford)

"They say, 'If you've got it, flaunt it'. Well, obviously Clare Short can't flaunt it."

Nikkala (21, from Middlesex)

23 August 2004

Today, 'Shell' has emerged from the Big Brother house with a shot at celebrity, and chooses to use the opportunity to get her tits out and slag off critics of Page 3:

"Those who sneer at Page 3 lack intelligence. It's beautifully-shot and tastefully pioneered the celebration of the female form. In many ways it emancipated women, letting them exploit their assets, earn cash and keep control. I see it as a modern art form."

Shell (23, from Glasgow)

11 January 2005

Nikkala reportedly brands a college principal's alleged decision to ban The Sun from their campus as "a disgrace" and adds:

"I just can't understand the thinking behind this petty-minded move. Page 3 is just harmless fun and it helps brighten up the day for a lot of blokes. Surely she must have better things to do with her time."

Nikkala (22, from Middlesex)

15 September 2006

On 12 September 2006, Clare Short expressed her shame and disappointment about the conduct of the Blair government, and announced that she would not be standing at the next general election.

Today, Keeley is reported to be "over the moon" that "MP Clare Short is on the way out" and says:

> "Page 3 girls will be glad to see the back of her -
> mind you, who'd want to see the front of her."
>
> *Keeley (19, from Bromley)*

Clare Short later resigned from the Labour party whip, and continued to serve as an independent MP until her retirement in April 2010.

29 December 2006

Today we are informed that "smart Sam," new topless model on the block, "has four A-levels - and has no time for people who think models aren't brainy":

> "It is a stupid stereotype that Page 3 girls are
> thick. I hope to prove people wrong."
>
> *Sam (21, from Sale)*

14 May 2009

Sam is reportedly "fuming that the Ministry of Defence are banning troops from looking at our beauties"; it is unclear if by 'beauties' she means the models generally or boobs specifically.

The Sun has reported that "po-faced bureaucrats have blocked Page3.com from military browsers, leaving Our Boys with no way to admire their favourite pin-ups," so it's all up to smart-girl Sam, who "paid a morale-boosting visit to the forces in Afghanistan last year" to make the strongest case possible for digital tit access for 'Our Boys':

> "If Defence Secretary John Hutton really is a friend of
> the troops, he'll overturn this silly ban immediately.
> All it does is appease the PC brigade."
>
> *Sam (23, from Manchester)*

Prepare yourself: you are almost at the end of the book, and we are very nearly done here.

I've resisted including a chapter of 'Conclusions', because I would much prefer that you arrive at your own on this one.

I thank you for your time, and leave the last word to the charming Rebekah Wade/Brooks, in her own voice (and under her own name), with the complete and unexpurgated version of the quote that appears at the very beginning of this book.

I believe it's important that her spirited defence of Page 3 back in the day be appreciated in total, and in context, before we all sign off and go home.

Cheers, all.

Tim Ireland

Short and fat

Page Three girls say their arch-critic Clare Short is just "jealous"

They also call her "fat and ugly"

And who are we to disagree with their verdict?

Page Three girls are intelligent, vibrant young women who appear in the Sun out of choice and because they enjoy the job.

Unsurprisingly, millions of our readers - men and women - enjoy looking at them.

If Ms Short ran our world it would be time to move to Mars.

Rebekah Wade
Editorial (full)
The Sun, 14 January 2004

www.ingramcontent.com/pod-product-compliance
Lightning Source LLC
Chambersburg PA
CBHW072204280526
45788CB00002B/872